CARPE COLLEGE!™

"Seize your <u>WHOLE</u> college experience."

For recent high school grads and those who love 'em.

Written by
Mike Metzler

Illustrated by
Kyle Labriola

Woodsman Press
Fairport, New York

Carpe College!
Seize Your Whole College Experience

Copyright © 2014 by Michael Metzler

Woodsman Press
Fairport, New York

Cover and book design by Qwurk Communications, Inc.
Illustrations by Kyle Labriola (www.kylelabriola.com)

ISBN 978-0-9899199-9-9 (Paperback)
ISBN 978-0-9899199-8-2 (ebook)

Library of Congress Control Number: 2013949747
Library of Congress Subject Headings:
College students
College freshmen
Education
Success
Universities and colleges

Dedication

This book is dedicated to my family. Obviously.
And to my students. Obviously.
Hmmm... Maybe it's a book about the obvious.

"Begin at once to live."

— SENECA

Carpe College

*"It does not do to dwell on dreams
and forget to live."*

— DUMBLEDORE

TABLE OF CONTENTS

Get Serious About Sleep
Lose the Laptop
Review & Revisit

Look, I Can See Your Breadth!
The Terrain
Stealing Strategy From Scouting (Be Prepared)

Thinking Inside the Box
A Place for Everything
Being Present

Tempus Fugit (More Latin?! You're Killing Me, Smalls!)
High School Happened. Embrace the Pace.
A Broader Plan
A Very Unique Gift
Oh Yeah. Don't Forget the Mantra
Sorry. One More Thing.

APPENDICES
Appendix A: The June Question (and a few more)
Appendix B: 'Don't Hate the Mate' Share Sheet
Appendix C: Weekly Planners
Appendix D: Checking In Charts
Appendix E: The Homestretch
Appendix F: Bolstering Your Breaks: Thinking Big
Appendix G: A Note to Struggling Students Whose First Year Goes Poorly
Appendix H: Commuter (And Community College) Care Package
Appendix I: Student Athletes
Appendix J: FREE Advice From Former First-Years
Appendix K: 'Look It Up' Resources
Appendix L: A Very Potter Guide to College Stuff

About the Illustrator
About the Author
Your Notes

Introduction

MISERY & BLISS

"I've never done a single thing I've wanted
to in my whole life."

— SINCLAIR LEWIS, BABBITT

There are millions of miserable, middle-aged people in the world, and I'm assuming you don't want to end up like them. That's what this book is about: developing habits and a plan to become... well... not miserable.

Pretty lofty, eh?!

For many, college is the first real and significant step toward finding one's place in the universe, to 'following one's bliss,' as Joseph Campbell put it. (Look him up!) So, if you prefer bliss to misery, you'll need to embrace the college experience in all its glory. You'll need to have a sense of yourself, your goals, your strengths and weaknesses. You'll need to have an active approach to tackling schoolwork, meeting new friends, and expanding your horizons. You'll need to start dreaming your own dreams, rather than those of your parents. You'll need to develop keen internal radar that helps you distinguish between opportunities and distractions. You'll need balance. You'll need to learn to trust yourself, to forgive yourself, to get back on your horse and take some more risk. You'll need to reflect seriously and often on the question: "Who am I, where am I going, why and how?" And, you'll need to learn and commit to memory a mantra that I've developed to help guide you every step of the way:

"Know Thyself. Have a Plan. Assume No One Else Cares."

Mostly, though, you'll need to...

Carpe College!

(Oh yeah, and parents will want you to find a job, so we'll cover that, too.)

3

(PARENTS IN PARENTHESES)

"Lord, help me not to do for my children what they can do for themselves. Help me not to give them what they can earn for themselves. Help me not to tell them what they can look up and find out for themselves. Help me to help my children stand on their own two feet to grow into responsible, disciplined adults."

— MARIAN WRIGHT EDELMAN, *GUIDE MY FEET*

Before we truly begin to *Carpe College!*, we need to assign some roles and responsibilities.

Hey parents, yes you are part of the deal, and yes this book is for you, too. But it's time to move to the sidelines and be more... how shall I say? Parenthetical. This book ought to give your kids the confidence to manage their new collegiate lives, and it ought to give you parents the peace of mind that your kids are well equipped to 'own it' on their own.

You can no longer be those 'Ice Curling' parents, who run on ahead and sweep away all the trouble spots, so your child can have smooth sailing. Nope. If you've tried that, you can't do it anymore! You should be present, to a degree, but you're a tag-a-long. Think about it. You've been practicing for this all along by watching little league games, stage dramas and music recitals from afar, and now it's time to kick your spectatorship into high gear. There's a huge difference between being a safety net and being a puppeteer. You need to be the former.

Be enriching, not overbearing. If you encounter an interesting article about your kid's favorite musician, a good *TED Talk* related to their major, or a good lead for an internship, by all means, send it along. But mark it 'No Response Needed' or something else you've worked out to indicate that you're just throwing stuff their way, and they shouldn't feel obliged to get back to you. You could even just say, 'Hey, thank me at Thanksgiving.'

Don't worry. Of course, they're going to talk to you before that! You're just demonstrating how easy going you can be.... Right?!

Encourage from afar. Keep communication lines open by letting them know you're available when THEY need to call or text. Leave the ball in their court, and respect their new lives, schedules and demands. They will need (and want) to communicate with you, but they would like to do it on their terms and timeline. Please let them. Give them their space, and they will be stronger. You will be stronger. Kind of like free-range turkeys (or something like that).

So, parents, please proceed to your proper place...in (parentheses)!

★★★

Oh yeah, and if you 'borrowed' this book from your kid, please be sure to return it to its proper owner.

HOW TO USE
THIS BOOK

This book is about looking forward.

B y the time you're reading this, I'm guessing you already know which college you'll be attending. Leading up to that point, I'm guessing you already received plenty of advice about applying to college and choosing a college and getting into a college. I'm guessing you read some books, checked out some websites, took some campus visits and listened to a whole lot of advice from teachers, guidance counselors, parents and other kids. And I'm guessing that was a kind of 'fun' you'd never experienced before in your life. So, now that it's over, it's time to take a deep breath, relax, bask in the glory of all your hard work paying off, and begin to look forward.

A Caveat Before You Carpe. (What's with the weird Latin talk?!)

Essentially, this means that there's a warning before we begin, and that warning is…

Everyone who ever went to college will have an opinion about it.

Now, I'm just one guy with some thoughts, some ideas, some perspective to share. And, because I'm me, I think you should listen to me. But because I'm just one guy, you should listen to everyone else, too. The best strategy for you as a young person heading off to college is to reach out to as many people and resources as possible -- parents, aunts, uncles, teachers, older sibs, the neighbor a few doors down who's a couple of years ahead of you -- and listen to 'em all. Acknowledge that they ALL have value. Ask them how they selected their major and if they use it in their work today. Ask them about highlights and lowlights of their college years and what they would do differently if they could do it all over again. Note the similarities and differences in what you're hearing, tuck it all away in your memory bank, and take it with you to school. You'll try some stuff, learn from it, listen some more, and try again. You'll attempt to make sense of it from there, and you'll be making up your own mind through it all.

Welcome to the adult world of trying to figure it out as you go.

As for this book, treat everything you read in *Carpe College!* as fodder for examination and discussion. It's food for thought, grist for the mill, fat to chew, shit to shoot, hash to sling.... It's all fair game for debate and dissection. Your parents may not agree with some of my perspectives. They might think I'm an idiot. Perfect. More stuff for you guys to talk about. It's all fine. It's all good. Maybe Aristotle said it best: "It is the mark of an educated [person] to be able to entertain a thought without accepting it." Accept or don't accept.

What's important about reading this book and embarking on your college career is that you get to make it yours, and that you're the one doing the Carpe-ing.

Let us begin.

CARPE COLLEGE:
AN IDEA

"I wanted to live deep and
suck out all the marrow of life...."

— HENRY DAVID THOREAU

So, what the heck is *Carpe College!*? It's an idea. An approach. An M.O. A habit. A way of embracing everything college life throws your way – academics and the rest – and doing so with vigor. Or, as President Kennedy would have said, "with VIGAH!" It's also an exploration, a continual experiment, a series of tests and trials and the dipping of many toes into many different waters in an attempt to uncover who you are and how you fit. With others. With the world at large. With your own notion of who you'd like to become.

This is *Carpe College!*

It's being liberated and taking risks. It's being smart about managing those risks, not cowering before them, but recognizing that all the best learning comes from risk-taking and results. Risk-taking and results. Rinse. Repeat.

And, with your newfound liberty, you'll need to take some liberties. For starters, I've taken liberties with our Latin translation. Literally, *Carpe College!* means 'Seize the college!' Now, inciting riots won't get any of us anywhere, so let's simply settle on a fast and loose translation: 'Seize the college experience (in its entirety).'

To do so, there will be some assumptions:

Assumption #1: You've finished high school, and you've chosen to attend college.

If you're not a graduating (or graduated) high school senior, then you're not ready for this book. You need to be in the right mindset, ready and excited to head off to college. If you haven't yet had senior prom, or the girls' softball team is still finishing their season, drop this book and pick it up again when summer comes. Enjoy your high school stuff while you're there, and then come back to this later. In the meantime, if you wish, loan it to your parents and let them read it until school's out. Then you can read it after them, and there will be plenty for you guys to talk about. (That way, you guys can make fun of me together! It could be a great bonding experience for you.)

Assumption #2: You've done your homework.

If you've chosen to go to college, you've done your due diligence to determine that it's the best option for you. You've reflected on your own dreams and goals and see college as the best path toward that end. You've had deep conversations with your family to explore the cost-benefit economics of your choice. You've considered a 'gap year' (a year off) to find yourself, blow off steam, travel, serve your community, or explore your interests more fully before plopping down thousands of tuition dollars.

(NOTE: If you're like many, you've completely blown off this assumption, making an ass out of you and me.)

Assumption #3: You've considered other options.

You've considered the notion that, in today's digital era, a highly motivated young person can educate herself with plenty of low-cost, online offerings, from EdX and Coursera to Khan Academy to Semester Online or Open Learning Initiative (Look 'em up. And just look up 'MOOCs' while you're at it).

Or maybe you've dipped your mental toes into the scary yet titillating waters of UnCollege or a Thiel Fellowship (Look 'em up).

Assumption #4: You understand the difficult terrain.

Because you've done your homework, you realize that about half of all students who enter a four-year college do NOT graduate in even SIX years.

Assumption #5: After all of the above, you've decided on college!

Assumption #6: You don't want to miss the bliss.

The happiest and most successful people are those who heed Campbell's advice: Follow your bliss (i.e. Find out what makes you happy and spend your days doing that). If you already know what your bliss is, and you're locked into a major and a career path you KNOW you're going to love, there will still be plenty of other 'blissful' elements to your college life. If you don't know what 'your bliss' is, then you'll need to continue to explore, explore, explore throughout your college years. Try everything.

If you don't believe anyone will pay you to play baseball or to play your guitar, then you'll need to explore other (possibly related) options. For example, if you can't play baseball professionally, maybe you can:

- write about it
- broadcast it
- surgically repair players' shoulders
- crunch stats
- design ballparks
- run concessions
- be a team photographer
- become a general manager
- engineer new equipment (can you say 'lighter, more powerful bat?!)
- be a docent (look it up!) at the Baseball Hall of Fame

The same could hold true for you not-on-a-path-to-become-a-professional-musician musicians out there. *Rock-n-Roll Hall of Fame* historian, anyone?! Or music teacher or therapist or producer... You get the idea.

It's this last assumption that's most important really. If you're not interested in being happy, you've got me befuddled, and I'm not sure we should proceed (but feel free to keep reading if you wish).

To follow your bliss, you need to cast a wide net to find what makes you happy. And, while you should have been casting all of your life so far, it's likely that you haven't been too strategic about it. However, you can certainly choose to be more intentional about it now.

In fact, that's what *Carpe College!* is all about. Beginning the next phase of your life — the college phase — actively and intentionally seizing every moment and every opportunity in order to find, and ultimately follow, your bliss.

BEGINNING
AT THE
BEGINNING

"Do not become a mere recorder of facts,
but try to penetrate their origins."

— IVAN PAVLOV

Where to begin? Well, this is all about EDUCATION, after all, so let's start there. Notice I didn't say 'schooling.' Education can take so many forms, and, when you stop to think about it, every day is an education, whether you're near a school building or not. You can learn not to feed your dog birthday cake when you see what comes out his other end. You can learn that ingesting a spoonful of cinnamon or chugging a gallon of milk is never going to end well. You can learn that delaying gratification can result in lots of rewards. Just ask the kids in the famous 'marshmallow experiment.' (Look it up!)

Education is what you've been doing all your life because you're a naturally curious kind of animal. When you were a little tyke, you were curious about everything. You would wake up in the morning and look out your window with fascination and wonder. At breakfast you'd climb under your chair to see how it was made. Outside, you'd mess with frogs, make designs out of leaves, watch how rainwater ran down the street, and become utterly fascinated by clouds and birds and anything else in the sky. Back inside, God forbid if you got into the tool set, the baking supplies or your mother's make-up. You were going to make something special, and nothing could stop you! To complement your curiosity, you were energetic and engaged.

The problem is that we took that wonderfully natural, childlike curiosity and tried to institutionalize it. You went off to school with high hopes for

more wonder. However, much of institutional schooling centers around 'keeping a lid on things,' so there were orderly lines for the bathroom and rules about the volume of your voice and lots of concern about who was and was not seated properly in their chairs. We put you in boxy desks inside boxy rooms inside boxy buildings, staring at boxy whiteboards and boxy screens, and we called it 'School.' Now, some of this was just the nature of the beast. To get all those young people 'through the system,' we needed some of those institutional constraints. But we ran the risk of beating (or boring) all the natural curiosity out of you in the process.

In a very short period of time, you learned that there was an adult present, and that he or she would dictate the order of the day. So, on the day of the first snowfall, you didn't run to the window. You sat in your seat and, if you were lucky, the teacher gave you an outline of a snowman to 'color' (with a pile of black and white crayons). This, of course, was a portent of a more dire future: 'The Worksheet,' an institutional schooling mainstay. All students come to learn that their job is to show up and sit in that desk. Eventually, some teacher will pass out some worksheet, and all you have to do is complete it. The teacher will collect it, and you will forget it.

Unfortunately, some of you had high school experiences as mind-numbing as this. Teachers droned on, firing facts and figures your way, and if you were lucky, you'd get the beloved worksheet or a silly word scramble puzzle sheet to break up the monotony. On an extra special day (or if the teacher wasn't feeling well), you'd get to watch a movie. Blah. Blah. Blah. You got shuffled from one class to another, like Pavlov's dogs answering a bell. (Look it up!) But you weren't salivating in anticipation for your next class; you were suffering through. You'd think, I'll sit in the chair until some adult tells me what to do, or I'll play their game and complete the sheet they put in front of me. You were probably trying to be nice, grinning and bearing it, but over time, you may not have even realized what was happening. It's kind of like that old frog story. Toss a frog into a pot of boiling water, and he'll jump out. But if you toss him into a pot of warm water and slowly heat it to extremes, he'll boil to death because he doesn't notice the change around him.

So, what was this slow change? It was what all of this 'factory model' education did to you. It made you one of the most dangerous things imaginable when it comes to learning: *passive*. Your teacher would serve up that stuff, and you well-behaved darlings (with visions of following the rules to get into college) would smile and say, "Yes, teacher. That's a great worksheet!" But you didn't mean it. You didn't care about it. And you certainly didn't really learn from it in any deep and true way. You could retain enough to take the test or write the essay, but then that newfound knowledge left you, floating passively out into the ether. You did not engage in that 'learning process' to develop yourself into a knowledgeable person in each of your academic disciplines. You did so because you had some larger, far off goal (College? A job?), and you needed to jump through some hoops to get there. If they put something in front of you, you'd do it, but you wouldn't *really* think about it. You wouldn't *really* internalize it. You wouldn't *really* make it your own, make it a part of you, make it memorable to take with you forever. You took the test, and you forgot the s★★★ that was on it.

We all know that that's no way to live a life! And it's certainly no way to *Carpe College!*

Fret not. It's not your fault. The process, the machinery, did this to you. And there's no time to spend assigning blame. There's only time to right the ship.

It's time to put an end to that passive nonsense and reclaim the active learner, that curious 'toddler terror' you once were. Take some time to reflect on *every* instance of passivity in high school, every worksheet encounter, and re-invent a way that you could have made it more like 'toddler time,' a moment full of thrill and awe. Yes, your chemistry and history teachers should have done that in the first place, but it's *your* job now.

And it's your job from now on.

WOW,
THAT WAS HARSH!

That last chapter was a bit of a downer and a bit cynical, wasn't it?! And it probably doesn't apply to all of you. Surely, many of you were actually engaged and invested in your high school learning endeavors. Surely, some of you retained what you 'learned.' (Surely, some of you have seen *Airplane* and are quietly saying, "Don't call me Shirley!" Look it up!) So, if that last chapter employed too much hyperbole, simply ignore the exaggerations and use it as an invitation to reflect:

- Did you, at any time, become passive in high school?
- When, where and how did it happen?
- Was it preventable?
- Do you think you can you prevent it when you get to college?

Okay, enough with the hard dose of high school reality (or the hard dose of hyperbole, if you wish), and let's move on to more positive pastures of the college variety.

SWINGING FROM THE TRAPEZE AT THE COUNTRY CLUB

(aka More Metaphors Than You Can Shake a Stick At)

Some students arrive at college with the mindset that they are consumers. They have stepped into this establishment, laid their money on the counter, and they want to walk away with the goods and services they demand. "If I don't want to attend class some days, tough!" they'll say. "As long as I get the work done and perform well on the tests, then those professors should just do their jobs, earn that salary I'm paying for, and give me the grades I deserve."

Unfortunately, college is less like a mall and more like a country club. You apply to get in and they decide to accept you. Once accepted, you have to pay very expensive dues (tuition) and abide by certain policies, like taking certain core classes, following the student code of conduct, and adhering to the detailed expectations laid out on each professor's syllabus. You have joined a club. You are part of a community, which means you give and you get.

But the fact that you don't get to call all the shots doesn't mean you can't make the most of it. To lace another metaphor into the mix, imagine that, instead of a golf course, this country club has a circus trapeze with a safety net. Now, you have spent so much time, effort, and money trying to get accepted into the club, you don't want it all to come crashing down. You don't want to screw it up. You don't want to get hurt. So you worry about the safety net (academics, studying hard, getting good grades, etc.). You want it to be secure to ensure a good outcome. Of course, it's good to proceed with caution, but too much caution could become a detriment. Your intense desire for a great outcome might cause you to focus so much on the safety net (the books) that you never take a turn on that trapeze (the richness of the overall college experience). It's like that old proverb: "The perfect is the enemy of the good." A perfect academic career with little else is far from good. In the end this could actually undercut your success and long-term goals.

Carpe College! is about your entire college experience, about getting on that trapeze, hanging upside down, and maybe doing some flips. Guess what? You're going to fall. But it's going to be thrilling, and you're not going to get hurt. You'll get to pick yourself up and try again. There will be practice time and performances and, in the end, you'll be glad you spent some time flying through the air.

So, you need to be active and intentional about having enriching experiences throughout your college years. Our mantra deals with ensuring you have a good safety net: know thyself, have a plan, and assume no one else cares. However, spending as much time as possible swinging from that trapeze can be part of the plan, it can help you discover more about yourself, and you get to control where and when and how you swing.

Make it thrilling both inside and outside the classroom.

Learnin' ~~vs.~~ and Livin'

Carpe College

LEARNIN' AND LIVIN': AN INTRO

*"The mind is not a vessel that needs filling,
but wood that needs igniting."*

— PLUTARCH

A simple way to break down the entire college experience is to separate it into two parts: Learnin' & Livin'. (As you can see, I made the mistake of inserting 'versus' on the previous page, but I caught myself.) Of course, when you're learning, you're living, and when you're living, you're learning. The two are far too intertwined to attempt to separate them or pit them against each other and, most of the time, you wouldn't want to do so. They're like a perfect peanut butter and jelly sandwich – to be experienced as one.

However, for our purposes, and to help us zero in on specific elements of college life, we will separate them. It's kind of like your jock and theater friends sitting in the cafeteria. They both keep life interesting, and you wouldn't want a day without 'em, but things tend to work better when they occupy separate tables.

So, there's the learning part ("It's what you're there for," everyone will say), and there's the living part (what they might call "college life"). We'll say that 'learning' includes the serious academic, book-learning part of the college experience, and 'living' includes the other learning parts of the college experience. Note that they **BOTH** include **LEARNING**.

If you're having trouble envisioning how these two work together, simply turn on your TV for a college football game and watch the goofy body-painted students carrying on in front of the cameras. Then stick around long enough to see the schools' finely produced commercials airing during halftime. Can the same student who's conducting cellular research in the honors program be seen at the game drenched in blue body paint, jumping up and down like an overly caffeinated maniac?

The straight answer is yes. It's all about balance.

Actually, it's not as simple as saying, "Yeah, I'll balance my academics and the other stuff." To truly *Carpe College!* you need to recognize that both elements of the college experience are valuable, and you need to ACTIVELY and INTENTIONALLY attend to both. Being completely honest with ourselves (and poring over the research), we would have to admit that there is plenty of 'living' (i.e. play) in the realm of academic learning. It should be fun, after all! And we would also recognize that there's a serious personal development component to our non-academic pursuits.

So, in order to seize the opportunities in both realms, we need to value and pursue them both. To guide that pursuit, here's that mantra again:

"Know Thyself. Have a Plan. Assume No One Else Cares."

This mantra encompasses all aspects of college life – both the learnin' and the livin'. You can know yourself in terms of how good you are at taking lecture notes, or whether you make friends easily. You can have a plan for studying during the week and another for meeting people in your dorm. You can assume no one else cares whether you fail a test or whether you bought your ticket to the football game. Whatever it is, the mantra can be your guide.

Revisit it often. Reflect upon it often. Write it on the palm of your hand weekly if it will help. (This assumes you'll be washing yourself at least weekly, and the ink will fade – let's hope that both are true.)

LEARNING:
THE ACADEMIC PART
(AKA 'THE GAME')

"Play the game for more than you can afford to lose. Only then will you learn the game."

— WINSTON CHURCHILL

"Knowledge is good."

— ANIMAL HOUSE

Okay, just after I get done trying to break down Learning and Living, I've now complicated matters by calling academics 'The Game.' Well….Tough! Welcome to the wonderfully gray and garbled world of higher learning. It's lofty intellectual pursuits, and it's the Less-Than-Hallowed Halls of Hackademia. It's a game, and it's not a game. Deal with it.

If academic life (ahem… learning) is to be fun, and many believe it should be, why not turn it into a game? Moreover, if higher education has become institutionalized with lectures and time schedules and assignments and grades and goals (not to mention transcripts and diplomas and people 'on the outside' who will judge you on how well you've done), then developing strategies for 'playing the game' might be in order. If you've developed strategies in Monopoly for putting up hotels and playing your 'Get Out of Jail Free' card, and you've developed strategies for scoring well in your favorite video game, then why wouldn't you employ some of that wonderful training, and the valuable skills you've garnered along the way, to play a bigger, more important game?!

A sound strategy begins by revisiting our mantra:

"Know Thyself. Have a Plan.
Assume No One Else Cares."

KNOW THYSELF

"The unexamined life is not worth living."

— SOCRATES

Knowing thyself is a significant part of surviving and thriving in college. Who have you been? Who are you now? Do you plan any immediate changes to adjust to your new college surroundings? Who do you wish to be in a year? In four years? In life? It's a good idea to explore this stuff as it relates to your 'academic self' in the context of the 'academic game.'

For the most part, you should be pretty well-versed at playing the academic game because you've been doing it for twelve years or so. The teaching-learning process looks about the same in any institutionalized setting. There are people in charge of facilitating your learning. You'll like some of 'em. You'll hate some of 'em. Some will inspire you. Some will bore you. The same will hold true with the courses you take. You'll like 'em, you'll hate 'em, you'll sleep through some, and you'll fondly remember others. But there will be one constant among all these teachers and classes: GRADES. You will get 'em at the end, and they will follow you forever.

Your true purpose for attending these classes is to learn, to gain wisdom and insight, and to secure knowledge that will stay with you and allow you to build upon it in your future. But the college 'game' is still played with grades, as crass as that may be, and your *short-term* success will be measured by them. Knowing your strengths and weaknesses, knowing how you function best, and quickly identifying the kinds of learning environments you're in (including the rules that govern each) put you in a great position to win the game.

TO HELP YOU 'KNOW THYSELF,' HERE ARE SOME IDEAS FOR REINTRODUCING YOUR 'SELF' TO YOURSELF:

Regularly 'check-in' and ask yourself, "Who am I? Where am I going? Why? How?"

This can be weekly, monthly, at the end of each term, or after a big test. It's a great way to assess how you're managing your long-term, big-picture goals (are you keeping your eye on the prize?), as well as the day-to-day perspective of HOW you're going about reaching those goals.

If you want to be a mechanical engineer, do you really know what it takes to become one? Have you done any research to see how and where a mechanical engineer might work? Have you met any in person? Have you spent a day with one? If you chose it as your major, take an HONEST and HARD look at the kind of investigation you've done to arrive at your decision. If you're still over 20% uncertain (as determined by your very own private 'I'm being completely honest with myself' scale), then it's time to explore some more. (More on how to do this later.)

On another front, how are you doing in Calculus and Physics? Do you see any connection between these classes and your major and career aspirations? Keep looking for one. If you got 83% on that last test, have you done a 'post mortem' to determine HOW you lost 17%? Was part of it carelessness; you knew the material but worked too quickly through the test? How much of it was content you didn't have a handle on? Have you stopped in to go over it one final time with the professor to ensure that you'll understand it for life? After all of that, have you tweaked your approach to learning, so that you can avoid missing out on that 17% again? Think on these things.

Reflect back on your high school academic successes.

What were your strengths and weaknesses? Did certain classes come easier than others? Why? Were you more motivated? Did you like the teacher or the material? Was it presented in a way that made sense to you? Were there any very challenging courses where you found success because of the factors listed above? Did you have challenging courses where *your* approach to learning the material worked particularly well? If so, focus on these. *You* must have employed some strategies that helped *you* succeed. Write 'em down and remember them. Odds are likely that you'll find these strategies useful again.

What's Your Function?!

Do you have any insight into *how* you function best? Were you a better student when you were busy with sports or other activities? Was this because you were forced to manage your time well? Did you read or do your math homework on the bus on your way to the game? Did you get any studying done when you hung out with teammates waiting for the bus, or was it easier to study alone? Did you find a special teacher who let you hang out in her room after school to get your work done? Did you find some other special place in your school building where you worked most effectively?

The same questions hold true for your home. Did you study while in bed with the covers pulled up? Was there music playing? Were your Facebook friends chiming in? Was texting taking up your valuable time as the minutes ticked along? There's plenty of research out there suggesting that these are *not* good ideas. (Look it up!)

What happens when 'the institution' can't bend to your style & preference?

If you function best when you have a very engaging and entertaining teacher who keeps you active in the classroom with lots of interaction, and who complements that environment with really interesting assignments, what happens to you when you end up in a class that doesn't provide those enticements? What if you get a really boring teacher, who just lectures and throws slides up on the screen, and the assignments are just plodding along through the textbook?

What if you like to see charts and illustrations and visual examples, and you like to work on projects and discuss issues, and that's how you learn best? What happens when you're in a class that offers none of this? Will *you* be able to adjust when the *institution* cannot?

Could you form a study group for discussions? Could you re-work your class notes, so that they are in a form that suits your learning, by creating your own visual elements? Could you create your own project or examples for every big concept shared in class?

Most important, did you try any of these strategies in high school? If not, you may need to consider if they might work for you when you find yourself in such circumstances.

Have you been lying to yourself?

Are you one of those students who got through high school without studying or using a planner or, as one guy told me, without carrying a single notebook his senior year? Or, blowing off any work until you crammed for an exam and still ended up with a decent grade? Or, worse yet, did you celebrate that 'accomplishment' with your friends and get a good chuckle, knowing all along that it wasn't too bright? While some of that might have 'worked' in some settings and may have given you a good story to tell, let's get real. There's not a chance any of that will work at college. And, if high school was supposed to serve as 'practice' for college, then you weren't practicing what you should have. Especially senior year! Did you get sucked into the "Senior Slide" where you didn't practice any good student success habits? In the year before the biggest academic leap of your life, did you take the year off, making the leap all that much larger? If so, that's like a team earning a berth in the tournament championship and then taking a week off before the big game.

Not wise!

In the end, knowing thyself could also be called "growing thyself" because, of course, you're still emerging as a young adult. It's about understanding where you have come from, recognizing it for what it was, and setting about making it better. If you adopt this approach with a dose of humility, you will continue to grow and enjoy watching your emerging self. You will also put yourself in a great position to develop your own strategic plan, which is the next part of our mantra.

HAVE A PLAN

"However beautiful the strategy,
you should occasionally look at the results."

WINSTON CHURCHILL

G ood ol' Winston is right. Results obviously matter. But you're not in a position to look at results yet because you're just starting out. So, consider that many successful students have come before you and developed some 'beautiful' strategies you can emulate. Consider that you can pick and choose what might work for you. And consider that if you consistently remind yourself that the results do matter, and you work your way back from there to develop your strategies, good things should happen....beautifully.

CONSIDER "THE JUNE QUESTION."

Having a plan is all about envisioning your goals and figuring out an approach for getting there in the end. I always talk to my students about "The June Question." I point out that in June following their first college year,

they will have begun their summer activities, and they will find themselves in a social gathering with family or friends. Inevitably, someone is going to come up to them and ask, "Hey, how was your first year at college?" My students typically nod in agreement that they're sure to be on the receiving end of that question, so I simply ask, "What would you like your answer to be?"

Now, this all seems quite basic, but when I'm meeting with students in the fall of their very first year of college, thinking about June is often the last thing on their minds. Although many students have some vague notion of what they'd like a successful college experience to be, very few have tried to put it into a single sentence response.

So, bringing it up helps to focus on some goals, and their responses cover some general terrain, such as "I'd like to say....

... I did well."
... I got good grades."
... I enjoyed learning."
... I was challenged."
... I made some good friends."
... my professors were good."
... I had fun."

Since they are typically surprised by the question, these lofty, yet vague, responses require some probing, and more digging helps them flesh out what their goals might become. When I ask them what 'doing well' or 'getting good grades' means, they begin to respond with more detail:

"Even though I know it will be hard, I'd like a 4.0."
"I need a 3.2 to keep my scholarship."
"I want to make the Dean's List." (Even though many don't know the criteria yet)
"I want A's and B's."

This approach of planning ahead to imagine what you'd like to be able to say is a lot like visualization exercises psychologists have used for years to encourage people to envision themselves executing a successful performance. Basketball players visualize scoring the game-winning basket. Gymnasts visualize sticking their landing. Stage actors visualize a performance that brings the crowd to its feet. Politicians visualize rallying the crowd with an elegant and forceful speech. "The June Question" is simply the same approach applied to students.

So, if you're visualizing your prized performance, you are probably interested in keeping your eyes on the prize, and "The June Question" is a good starting point for identifying what that 'prize' is. For the even longer term, why not make a list of responses for "The Grad Question," those things you'd like to be able to say you will have accomplished at graduation time, and then you can work your way back from there. It could be in the form of Q & A or you could write up a sort of 'bucket list' for your college years. Either way, it might include stuff like this, working from the macro to the micro:

Q: How was college?

A: Great. I made Dean's List all 4 years w/ GPA of 3.5

Q: How was your senior year?

A: Great. I got an internship for 1st semester, and I did it in Spain, which helped with my Spanish.

Q: How was last semester?

A: Great. I got to help one of my professors with her research, and I got a leadership position on the Campus Activities Council.

Q: How was last week?

A: Great. I got my paper and big lab done early, giving me extra time to rehearse for my choir audition, and it cleared up my weekend, so I can go to the game and Saturday parties.

This last question begs the next question: "How do you make a 'good week' happen?" Well, the devil is in the details, and what follows can help you navigate those detailed waters.

THE FAMOUS FORMULA
(AKA SMELLS LIKE TEEN FREEDOM):

When we talk about students tackling school and managing their time, there seems to always be reference to the famous formula:

> *For every hour spent in the classroom, students should spend two hours studying outside of class (some even say three hours).*

Most people would be hard-pressed to tell you who came up with this formula, but *everyone* seems to have bought into it. And you probably should, too.

It's saying, for example, that if you take a course load of five three-credit-hour courses, you should be spending 30 hours per week studying (reading, homework, reviewing notes, previewing, etc.) outside of class.

Now, this may seem like foreign terrain for most recent high school grads. First, many have *never* put in that kind of studying in their lives.

Second, high school is actually geared more toward class time. That is, most high school students spend about six hours per day in class (about 30 hours per week) and less than that on homework. At college, students spend closer to 15 or 20 hours in class each week, yet the outside-of-class expectations are much higher.

This is the great 'turning of the tables,' and it causes great difficulty for students transitioning from one setting to the next. High school teachers spend a lot of their breath preaching to their students about how hard college will be. "Just wait till you get to college," they'll say. "You'll be in for a rude awakening." But they're thinking about 'The Formula.' Their audience, passive high schoolers who 'do school' but don't always do homework, have a totally different perspective. They believe most of schooling happens in the classroom, and homework is often busywork they've learned to mindlessly power through. They typically only care about one or two subjects, and the rest are just jumping through someone else's hoops. So, they devote some time to this 'schooling,' but they don't devote *themselves* to it in the hopes of learning and retaining for life.

These students get to college expecting rigor. They know they were just playing games in high school, but college will be different. They do want to learn. They do want to embrace learning for life. But, upon arrival, they encounter fewer hours each week in the classroom and very little 'busy-work' for homework. In fact, in some classes, they may not have their first assessment for several weeks. If they're still in high school mode, and no one is putting a specific homework assignment in front of them, it feels like nothing but *freedom*. (Insert Frisbee on the lawn here!)

This is why 'The Formula' matters!

'The Formula' says, in essence, block out the time each week to devote to learning, and then *fill* that time. If you passively wait for someone to tell you what to do, you're too late, and the train will have already left the station. So, assuming you *really* want to learn and *really* want to comprehend and retain what's being taught, proceed accordingly:

- Follow the Formula: For every 1 hour in class, devote 2 hours outside of class (often *before* class) to homework and studying.

- To use that 'out of classroom' time effectively, you need to plan it and use it wisely.

- Assume every test will be a recall rather than recognition test. A recognition test is like a multiple-choice test. You can simply recognize the right answer when you see it among other choices. When you've become accustomed to taking many standardized, multiple choice tests, you can develop poor study habits, poor test preparation, because you simply review your notes recognizing the stuff you've seen before. You don't really force yourself to understand it fully, believing instead that you'll "know it when you see it."

   A recall test is like an essay test. You need to recall everything from memory, from scratch. Preparing for a recall test requires much more time and dedication, and that's how you'll use all that studying time you've set aside with 'The Formula.' The test of whether you know the course material or not is a simple 'white page' test. If you can take out a blank sheet of white paper and, starting from scratch, define and lay out all the major ideas, concepts, examples, illustrations and applications, then you're ready.

   If not, it's back to the drawing board.

   This Recall vs. Recognition approach requires lots of *time* to pore over your course material. 'The Formula' sets aside that time. And, it's important to understand that *any* discussion about having a quality approach to academics will require a discussion about *time management*.

They are inextricably linked.

Here's our first crack at addressing that link...

WHAT'S YOUR 'EMO'?

Early in the year, I ask my students what EMO is, and we chuckle a bit about trying to define that pop-culture mystique. I think I've come to the conclusion that EMO is a lot like Supreme Court Justice Potter Stewart's famous take on obscenity: "I know it when I see it."

But in our case, we're not talking about tight jeans, indy music, and hair in your eyes. We're talking about the students' Effectiveness M.O. (EMO). I ask them what 'modus operandi' (way of operating, or M.O.) they use to be an effective student and person. That is, "What system do you use to *effectively* keep track of your life?"

Some students use a weekly planner similar to the one many high schools provide. Many colleges provide these at orientation, as well. (Hmmmm... Maybe there's a good reason these educational institutions continue to hand these out for free. Maybe they're a good strategic tool. Maybe they're more valuable than simply a collection of ads in the back. Oh wait, and they come with a campus map?! And info on practically *every* aspect of student life?! That might be useful.)

Though I have trouble imagining why anyone would veer away from this tried and true helper, I recognize that everyone is different, and college is about being open-minded, after all. So, there are plenty of other EMO's to go around. Some students use Post-it Note systems, where the notes are in their planner or stuck to their dorm room desk and then systematically moved and removed. Some use a white board above their desk. Some use one of those big blotter desk calendars. And some use an intricate combination of each method. Some students, as you might imagine, have even vaulted feet first into the 21st century and employ a digital system of online calendars synched with smart phones to keep track of their busy lives.

Then there are those students who use an age-old method from the pre-Gutenberg printing press era, called the "I just keep it all in my head" method. Now, I'm sure there are people who can do it, but in my experience, students who attempt this well-honed high school trick tend to crash and burn. Because they don't write stuff down, they miss assignments. They miss appointments. They miss social engagements. Such an approach can shape who you become in college. It can mean missing the additional details or announcements teachers make in class, or the changes in plans, or changes to the syllabus, and then those dastardly details come back to bite you. Mostly, however, it means missing out on the notion that one of the greatest beauties of *Carpe College!* is the invitation to think big. The opportunity to open your mind is what most college students have been waiting for their whole (just under two decades) lives!

And this begs an important question: Why in the world would you want to muddy your mind with minutiae, like your advisor's appointment or the deadline for your discussion board posting in your politics class, when you could be jotting that stuff down and freeing your mind to think about more interesting and important matters?! Isn't it better to expand your thinking with lofty thoughts than burden it with boring and mundane daily detail stuff? The answer, for most people, is a definitive *yes!*

So, here's just one guy's advice about an EMO that works:

1. **Get an academic planner to write in.** The free one from your school is fine, especially because the ads and the map and the 'fun facts' have been specially tailored for your campus. If your penmanship is barely legible, like mine, these planners can appear a bit small, though. So, you can find a bigger letter-sized model at any back-to-school sale. (And, of course, you are welcome to type into an electronic calendar if that's your preference!)

   The key to a good planner is that, when you open it up, you can see a 'week at a glance' and there should be another page that has a 'month at a glance.' The reason these are key features is because some wonderfully resourceful and organized folks who have blazed a trail before us realized this is a great way to plan. You can navigate from the big picture to the daily details, from the macro to the micro, from the "What do I need to accomplish this month?" to "What do I need to accomplish tomorrow?"

2. **Once you have a planner of your picking,** it's time to start penciling stuff in. Begin by visiting your school's academic calendar on their main webpage and write in *all* the important dates. These include holidays, of course, followed by deadlines for dropping and adding courses, and final exam week, among others. (Of course, if you're planner is provided by your school, all of these dates may already be loaded in for you.)

   Since you're probably pulling all of this info from your school's website, you might as well click over to their Student Affairs or Student Life page to get some more dates. Here they will have posted the big sports events, concerts, theater productions, Homecoming weekend, and a few of the big-name guest speakers coming to campus –

enough big stuff to get your social *Carpe College!* life started. Throw a handful of these big dates into your planner just so you can feel like you have...well...plans. (We'll come back to this later.)

3. **Bring your planner** to your orientation sessions when you meet your RA and learn all about campus organizations and intramurals and dorm activities. Once this stuff surfaces, just get it into the planner. Within a week or two, your planner ought to be filling up nicely, and you'll realize that it's a great tool to help you make the most of 168 hours. (That's right, that's the number of hours you have to not sleep away each week!)

4. **Now, back to the academic stuff...** After the big 'all campus' dates are loaded into your planner, it's time to personalize your planner with your own classes. During the first week of classes, sit down with every syllabus and transfer all the important class deadlines into your planner. Remember, that syllabus is in print, and it functions as the contract for your class. It is the 'bible' for all references related to your class, and if any questions or confusion emerge, it is the 'go-to' document to get everyone, literally, on the same page. Lock that important info into your planner!

5. **Take it to class,** of course, so when the professor announces that he's changing the deadline for the first essay, you'll be able to make a note of it. If you're not using a planner, but only a whiteboard or desk calendar back at your dorm, how do you plan to transfer this new deadline change? Have a plan! Use a planner.

A Final EMO Note: Many schools have online course management systems, where professors can post news, assignments, deadlines, etc. *Please do not* see this as an excuse to forgo your own planner. In these online systems, information is typically organized by course, and you'll need to mouse-click back and forth to get a handle on all of your courses. Your own personal planner has everything organized around you, your needs and your preferences.

So, if you utilize only your school's online course management system, and you want to get the lay of the land for what's due next week, you'd have to click around to all five of your classes. If you use your planner, you'd just open it to next week and see everything 'at a glance.'

An EMO 'combo-platter' utilizing *both* of these tools (your personal planner – either hardcopy or digital - *and* your online course management system) is my final recommendation. Enjoy!

A LIGHT SUNDAY NIGHT?

In my own years as a student, and working with current students, I've found that asking this question is a good barometer to gauge how your week is going. If Sunday night is packed with homework, and you're in for a stressful haul just to get everything finished so you can get more work thrown at you come Monday morning, then your approach might need some tweaking.

Imagine this: Sunday night begins with a fun and relaxing dinner with your friends, then a movie or some games, and early to bed with a chapter in a good book (not a textbook!) so you're well-rested for the week.

If you've never experienced it, you should consider it. Once you get past your "Isn't that the way old people live?" reaction, you'd be surprised how quickly this gains appeal with college students after they've put in a couple months at school. If they could ease into their week instead of feeling stressed about starting again on Monday, they would jump at the chance. And many make significant adjustments in their planning and time management in order to create a 'Stress-free Sunday night.' The problem is that it takes many weeks, sometimes months, for students to learn this lesson the hard way. But once they've tried it, they adopt it because they know it's healthier all around.

Why not consider planning this into your EMO right from the outset?! You'll thank yourself (and me) later.

THE FIRST-YEAR TESTING GROUND

During your first year of college, you will experience much that is new academically. Your schedule and campus will be very different from high school, your professors may have dramatically different expectations than your high school teachers, and the course material may be more rigorous than high school. (Or not – sometimes students feel unchallenged by their first-year foundation courses.) Regardless, you will be engaged in an ongoing 'feeling out' process of figuring out what the academic demands are and how your approach is working. My advice is twofold:

Use the ENTIRE first year as a testing ground.

Try your EMO and get results. Then adjust and try again. It's possible that it will require a full year to gain certainty that you've got a good approach. The goal is to arrive at the end of your first year with the confidence to say, "I've experienced everything they could throw at me over an entire year, I've tested and adjusted my approach, and I'm now ready to hit the ground running next fall with very little learning curve about HOW to play this college game."

Maintain an open mind.

It's quite possible that your approach to first semester will work well, and you'll have a successful first semester. This does NOT mean that you've conquered college! It's quite possible that the courses during your first term just happened to be foundation material designed to get a collection of first-year students from various academic backgrounds all up to speed and on the same page. So, maybe much of that stuff could be review for you. That probably will NOT be the case for your second term. Much could change after your first term, so don't presume that you've figured it all out after that. KEEP TESTING. Or, to put it another way, hope for the best but plan for the worst. If you make it to spring with SEVERAL successful performances under your belt, then you're probably onto something.

FREE YOUR MIND & THE REST WILL FOLLOW

After listening to first-year students who have maintained open minds about their approach to academics and who keep tweaking their EMO, I've heard similar 'lessons' surface again and again. Maybe you can benefit from these:

A weekly plan is a plus.

By having a plan and putting it in writing, it's much easier to see how your time is used and where more time can be found. It also opens up MORE opportunities, allowing you to fit more life into your life! (Revisit all the EMO info for more on this).

Time between classes is NOT down time.

For many first-year students who have a three-hour break between classes during their first term, it's an invitation to head back to the dorm for napping, socializing or seeking out other distractions. After first-term grades tumble, many students realize that time can be spent much more productively during the week. Those three hours (or even one hour!) could be spent doing homework, re-writing notes, reviewing/previewing, meeting with professors or study partners, or thinking big about anything.

Geography matters.

Instead of heading back to their dorm room for a nap or socializing (a rookie tactic), wise and learned students (i.e. anyone who's survived first-term) will head to a quiet floor of the library, or some other favorite spot on campus, and dig in to their academic work. The space you select will have an effect on what you do in that space. Another way to put it is, "Location, location, location." Where you are often dictates what you do. What if you left your dorm room in the morning and didn't return until the evening? Imagine what you could accomplish throughout your day!

Ignite a spark.

Ideally, you'll love your course material and you'll love your instructor. But there may be times when you just don't care for one or the other or both. If you don't love your instructor, try to love the course content. If you don't love the content, try to find value in your instructor. If you don't like either, then treat it like a summer job. You're just in it for the paycheck, and that payoff is the course credit you'll earn at the end of the term. You know early on that it's not going to be a joyride, so you need a clear strategy with clear daily and weekly goals for how you'll get through it. Toss in some rewards if that helps get you through. Plan to do your work for this course *first*, taking your tough medicine and getting it over with, or join a study group with classmates you really like, so it feels like less of a chore. If you were ever an athlete and you had to run hills in practice (or pick your most grueling drill), treat it like that. You hated it while you did it, but you could motivate yourself to battle through it because you knew there was a positive payoff at the end. It might be agonizing in the process, but it's worth it. This attitude takes a lot of mental toughness and an approach of breaking down the 'exercise' into small parts. If you're running hills, you're telling yourself, "just ten more steps... just five more steps!" If you're working on course material you don't care for, tell yourself, "Just one chapter tonight... just three pages of notes tonight!" It's a series of little battles with a big payoff at the end.

Of course, if this mental game is too much, there is the old adage that 'Smart people are never bored.' If you consider yourself a smart person, then you ought to be able to find something in the course content or the instructor that is compelling enough to engage your interest. And that should be enough to motivate you and get you through. Turn yourself into a critic. What's wrong with the professor or course? How could it be presented better? You'd be amazed how this kind of thinking engages your mind and begins to immerse you into the content of the course. That's a much better place to be than withdrawing to the periphery and avoiding everything related to the course because you find some of its aspects unappealing. Another good strategy, of course, would be to go see that professor more frequently than others. At worst, you'll force yourself to stay engaged with the person who is probably best suited to help. At best, you'll come to understand the material better through this extra time and effort.

In the end, you need to make it work. It's your journey. Buck up! You can do it.

Email should be easy.

Until further notice check your email daily. I know students love texting, but professors still like email. Until this changes, you would be wise to play the game on their terms. You do not want to miss an important email announcing a change for the time and location of your midterm exam.

Obviously, you tech savvy students can make sure your email is sent to your phone; however, I've seen students become frustrated when their email fills up with campus announcements that seem to simply get in the way. As a result, they make the mistake of eliminating or ignoring emails and end up missing that one important message from their professor. So, use whatever filtering system you need to sort through your emails, but be sure not to ignore any that relate to your courses.

Also, professional people are in the habit of checking their email daily, so it's a good habit to emulate. It's a must if you're dealing with people off campus for jobs or internships, too.

Ask. Ask. Ask!

The aforementioned wise and learned students also figure out the best way to develop and improve their own approach is to *ask others* what they do. Part of the testing process is to tap into all kinds of options. If a friend claims she has a great system for planning her day, try it. If someone else swears by his strategy for finding the best study spots on campus, follow his lead. If your academic support center offers a 'study tips' workshop, consider attending, just to see if you're the complete expert you thought you were. As with anything, emulate and adopt those aspects that work for you and, with a breath of kindness and minimal consternation, blow the rest away.

YOUR PREFRONTAL CORTEX ('PC') WALKS INTO A BAR.

The bartender asks if he wants a beer, but PC says to line up 3 shots. Holly asks if he wants to dance, but PC says dancing on the table might be more interesting. Bill thinks they should all go home to study for that Econ midterm. PC thinks a Star Wars marathon sounds more enticing.

Your prefrontal cortex, the part of your brain just behind your forehead, is sometimes called the 'executive suite' of the brain because it does some serious heavy lifting. It helps you solve-problems, plan ahead, prioritize, assess risks and rewards, manage your impulses, moods and emotions, and make judgments. Science has shown it is also not fully developed until one's mid-twenties when most people are through with college. While you're in college, your brain is still trying to figure out what it wants to be, the same way you're trying to discover yourself. So it's understandable that there might be some fumbling and stumbling, trial and error, and missteps during this period of your development. It might also be why many brain researchers (and others) suggest teens have a propensity to engage in less than mature behaviors or decisions, at times, and why car rental companies don't let you rent a car until way after you can legally drive or vote or drink.

For our purposes, however, from a 'know thyself' and 'have a plan' perspective, it makes sense to put systems in place to counterbalance where your prefrontal cortex might fall short. If you realize that your prefrontal cortex might be a bit flighty, then establishing goals and laying out clear plans and strategies to achieve those goals might make it easier to stick to them rather than letting good ol' PC just wing it.

Developing a system that's right for you is key to surviving and thriving in college. Keeping you and your interests front and center is the final aspect of our mantra and the focus of what follows.

ASSUME
NO ONE ELSE
CARES

"A man said to the universe:
'Sir, I exist!'
'However,' replied the universe,
The fact has not created in me a sense of obligation.'

— STEPHEN CRANE

BEING NICE

For demonstration purposes, let's just assume that everyone is nice. Your new college friends are nice people. Your old high school friends are nice people. Your parents are nice people. The guy down the hall offering free beer and Frisbee is nice (*and* the nice fall weather is nice), and the good-looking guy or girl from class who asks you for help with Political Science homework is nice.

They're *all* nice, and you should want to be nice in return.

However, you should remember, and remind yourself often, that their goals are not necessarily aligned with your goals. You have some semblance of a vision for your life, a plan to graduate, and an idea of what success should look like for your college career. You have a sense of what you need to accomplish in Chemistry class, how you'll need to get ready for that mid-term in three weeks, how that lab is due next week, and how you need to read that chapter before tomorrow's class.

That guy with the beer and Frisbee? You have to assume he doesn't care one lick about your plans. It's not that he's not nice. It's because he is not the 'Master of Your Destiny.' You are! And you need to be an advocate for yourself. If you can't do beer and Frisbee because you have to read those chapters, then you've got to tell him so. And, here's how you let him down easy: "Dude, I can't."

No whining about your workload. No made up excuses. Just "Sorry, Dude. I can't."

Wow. That wasn't too complicated.

Want to let him down easy *and* demonstrate that you're a nice person, too? Try this: "Dude, I can't. But I'll be ready at 4:00, and then we can grab some grub, too."

Impressive. Now you're Master of Your Destiny *and* a nice person!

MASTER THIS!

The *'Assume No One Else Cares'* part of our mantra is not really to make others look bad. It's designed, intentionally, as a harsh reminder that YOU must learn to become an advocate for yourself. YOU must be the one to keep your eyes on your prize. YOU must plan your life so you can play Frisbee AND study. That's your job and no one else's. If you can't learn to say NO to Frisbee guy, or NO to your parents, or NO to your girlfriend, or better yet, figure out a way to say YES while still following your own plan, then success may elude you.

If all this seems like a bunch of lame advice about how to keep people out of your life, it's really more about setting boundaries for your time and energy. You've been doing that for years (If you've ever ignored a text message until later, you know what I'm talking about). So, keep managing your own time and energy by setting these boundaries on your own terms. Of course, the better you plan, the easier it is to set boundaries because you'll be in control. And that will actually open up *more* social/leisure/play options as a result.

Everybody is in the same boat, and they WILL understand if you choose to bail out on some social fun in order to get schoolwork done. Some may give you grief or try to make you feel bad, but those are likely to be the ones stressed out on Sunday nights and panicked and cramming before tests. They will also be the ones secretly admiring you and envying your self-control. Everyone will really warm up to you if you have planned so well that you can get your work done AND be social, too. This would be a clear indicator that you're Master of Your Destiny.

PEBBLE IN THE POND

Instead of talking about keeping others at bay, let's consider scenarios where you want to reach out to others to assist in your academic success. Consider the image of a pebble tossed into a pond. The pebble hits, and water rings ripple outward in concentric circles. Guess what?! You're the pebble. And the rings are other people and resources all around you that can help you find academic success. Let's explore a few…

WAIT!! Before we do, this is where we need to realize that 'asking for help' does *not* mean you're sacrificing your newfound independence, and it does *not* mean that you are giving up your control as Master of Your Destiny. As a young person beginning your college career, you are not alone in possessing the hope that you're going to tackle this challenge on your own by mustering every fiber of your being to power through the obstacles and work harder than ever to emerge successfully on the other side. Everyone understands that you want to show the world what you're made of.

This is an EXCELLENT attitude, and you should not shed it!!

HOWEVER, too often, too many students misinterpret doing it 'on my own.' We need to rethink this approach and realize that reaching out to other people and using resources for help is, in fact, *retaining* control of your destiny *and* doing it on YOUR OWN terms. Consider this scenario:

> You've got to finish ten problems for Calculus class in two days. You get to the fourth problem, and it's a doozy. You spend 45 minutes trying to battle through it, but you're getting nowhere. So, you take a break, grab a snack, and regroup. Then you sit back down and put in another 45 minutes to no avail.

So far, so good. This is a fair and reasonable approach for someone who really wants to learn calculus and really wants to internalize the material for understanding and retention. The problem, however, is that it's not *just* about calculus. You've got other academic subjects and other aspects of your life to manage, too. So, your next move will be a watershed moment in determining your overall approach, your academic development, and your sanity.

Here's what you should NOT do: Dig back in for another 45 minutes.

Here's what you SHOULD do: Try something new.

Recognize that you *WERE* doing the right thing, initially, and that is supported by current brain research. You were struggling on your own with the material. This is what the experts refer to as 'playing' with the material, and it is a clear way to come to understanding and retention. Without a doubt, there is glory and value in such individual struggle. However, you hit a wall. There is a point of diminishing returns, a point at which you must decide to 'fish or cut bait.' And, I've determined (in all my 'expert' walking around life, backed only by observation, very little research, and only reason and practicality as my guide) that this point is around the 1½ hour mark. If you've put in this much struggle and effort ALONE, know that it was valuable. But also recognize that continuing down that track will become less valuable as every minute ticks by. You will become less lucid, less capable, and less interested in success if you continue to struggle much more on your own.

You could put your current work aside, move on to something else, and revisit it later. This is a viable option, it might work, and you should feel free to try it. But, here's another thought…

Begin reaching outward to those 'ripples of resources' you're surrounded by, my little pebble!

It's time to get up and take a walk down your dorm floor to find anyone, and I mean ANYONE, who might be able to help. If Calc Whiz Kid Wally isn't around, try someone else. If the dorm's a ghost town (or, better yet, if you're in the library), then use that handy little texting device to put the word out that you need some help from your peers. If you end up needing to wait for their response, then move on to the next ripple outward: that whole Internet thing. Start surfing for online tutorials (from Khan Academy or elsewhere) that might be able to walk you through, and get you past, your mathematical obstacle. If you come up dry, reach out to the campus math help service (most have 'em). Walk over there and find a tutor. Or text the teaching assistant (TA) from class to see if he or she can help. (Feel free to reverse the order of these ripple resources, of course, or shuffle them up into any order you see fit. Just let 'em work for you.)

Following this approach, you'll probably find the help you need to get you through. However, there's one more resource, one more outer ripple, you haven't tapped into yet: your professor. While you may not have had to reach that far for this single problem, it would be wise to follow up with the professor just to be sure you've got it right. Definitely, drop in the next day during the professor's office hours just to double check your work. (How's that for a punny math mantra? Double check your work! I crack myself up.)

So, my little pebble, there is nothing wrong, and much that is right, about reaching out for assistance in order to find success. **REMEMBER: You did *not* sacrifice your independence.** *You* struggled hard. *You* gave it a fair shot. *You* determined that any more time spent on one problem would not result in quality or get you closer to *your* goals. *You* wisely *chose* to reach out for assistance, which, by the way, resulted in *your* learning. And *you* attained what you set out for in the end: successful understanding of the course material that you will remember and retain for good. All of this was done on *your own* terms. *You* made an *independent* decision about how to proceed to reach *your* goals. It was all *YOU!*

(Despite the above emphasis on *you*, schools intentionally provide resources so that students won't suffer alone and fall behind. Need I say it again? Use 'em.)

HERE ARE A FEW MORE 'RIPPLE' CONSIDERATIONS:

Study partners or groups. These make sense from a brain research standpoint because conversing and working with others means you are 'playing' with the material in myriad ways. These groups help break up the monotony. They're efficient because questions surface and get ironed out much quicker than 'flying solo.' Plus, they can lead to some new friends and nice social opportunities after the studying is done.

One caveat: The best way to partake in a study group is if EVERYONE in the group agrees to 'struggle' with the material BEFORE coming to the group. By 'playing' with the material on your own, you develop a better un-derstanding of the concepts as well as the trouble spots. This puts everyone on a better learning plane once they arrive at the group. You can determine what everyone knows and review that material quickly. Then you delve into trouble areas and help each other. This makes for a very efficient use of time. Moreover, if you have a complete understanding of something that others find difficult, you get the opportunity to 'teach' them, and brain research suggests that this is an excellent way to solidify your own understanding. A traditional medical school approach suggests that the best way to truly know something is to:

"See one. Do one. Teach one." (Feel free to insert 'several' for 'one.')

You *see* a concept presented in class or through reading. You *do* it through homework/practice on your own. You *teach* it in a study group. It's often the teaching part that gets ignored, but it's really where the rubber meets the road in terms of understanding. If you can teach someone, then you truly know it. *(NOTE: If you can't find a group, then take out a white sheet of paper and 'teach' it to your imaginary friend by writing the concept out from scratch. If you can successfully get the idea and all its parts and processes down on the paper, then you know it.)*

But, do the study group. It's *way* more fun!

The A's Have It! If you're still concerned, my little pebble, about reaching out for help, maybe I can entice you with grades. You want good grades? Then reach out to those who can help you get those grades. Let's imagine that you're great at the humanities, social sciences and liberal arts, but math is an ongoing struggle. You can understand the material, but the process for getting there is slow and deliberate. Your friend down the hall, Whiz Kid Wally, is the reverse. He's a math whiz, who loves things black and white, but all the abstraction and gray of other subjects drives him nuts, and he needs more time to get a handle on those areas. *Both* of you are bright, and you'll both garner an understanding of your 'difficult' subjects in the end. But the process and the pace will differ.

Speaking of the end, let's say that you'd like to get an 'A' in Calculus this term. So, you struggle and play with the material as we mentioned earlier. Then you turn to Whiz Kid Wally as one of your ripple resources when you need help. Let's say that Wally ends up tutoring you week to week, plus you have regular chats and check-ins with your professor, and you attend all the TA's review sessions before the exams. When grades arrive, you've earned your A. It may have been a struggle with much wailing and gnashing of teeth, but you got an A. Guess what? Wally got an A too. For him it was a breeze. But guess who doesn't know that? Any jobs recruiter or grad school looking at your transcript. You got an A, and Wally got an A. It's right there in Wally's favorite colors, black and white. That's it. You BOTH got A's.

Are you some sort of fraud? NO! You're not pulling the wool over anyone's eyes. Though it was a struggle, you learned and retained the material.

In the end, if someone asks if you can understand and perform calculus, the answer will be the same as Whiz Kid Wally — Yes! And the same will hold true for him in his 'gray' classes (where he probably got some help from you).

It's what biologists call a symbiotic relationship. It's all perfectly natural!

Pre-Paid Support. Nearly all campuses have a center for academic support. This operation runs tutoring services, math and writing help centers, 'successful student' consulting, and anything else that will help students reach their full potential. It is a resource that's already paid for with your tuition dollars (for most schools), and it is staffed by folks who have plenty of experience understanding students' academic challenges and developing strategies for successfully navigating them. Need help with an essay? Visit the writing center. No dorm mates around to help with Calc? Visit the math help lab. They help with most academic stuff, and you're already paying for it. Not using it would be like paying for a cell phone plan, but using smoke signals instead.

Here are some other areas where they can help:
- Time management
- Motivation & procrastination
- Organization strategies
- Study skills
- How to read a textbook
- How to take notes
- Preparing for exams
- Coping with test anxiety

The Bottom Line: Get help when needed. Get good grades. Get on to what's next. There's lots more college to be carpe'd.

A POTENTIAL PROBLEM: TEAM PROJECTS?

So, after all this talk about using your Pebble in the Pond resources and mastering your domain to control your own destiny, there's still a burning question: "How can I be in control if I end up working on some team project with others who don't pull their own weight? (Don't THEY end up controlling MY destiny, then?)

Fair question(s)! But the less-than-palatable answer is that the ONLY way to control your destiny is to control it. Here are some suggestions for controlling it in a team project context:

1. Set and agree to goals, timetables, communication tools

(phones, email), team etiquette, and members' responsibilities FIRST.

It's a good idea for everyone on any team to share their strengths and weaknesses during your first meeting. This affords you the opportunity to assign responsibilities and to get everyone into their comfort zone. Those who are good at art can be in charge of the visuals for your presentation. Those who are good organizers can set your timeline and checkpoints. The good writers can write your report. If this works cleanly, then everybody gets to do something they like. It may turn out, however, that there are some responsibilities no one wants. Maybe nobody wants to write the report. If so, then you might need to break up this unpopular task and assign everyone a piece of it, and maybe the good writers can edit these pieces.

The key to this first phase is to divide and conquer the many facets of the project and to do it equitably and/or fairly while giving everyone some input and choice.

Once you've determined who's doing what and by what deadline, the person setting the timetable and checkpoints should draft a plan and share it. Everyone should discuss it, offer suggestions, and then agree to lock it in with specific checkpoints and deadlines for everyone. As much as you may rely on electronic communications and sharing of documents, sometimes there is no substitute for face-to-face meetings. Everyone is busy, so too many meetings can wear thin. Therefore, the few meetings you agree to hold should be sacrosanct and untouchable. Check your calendars, commit to the meetings, and make sure you get there (with your responsibilities met). Members missing meetings because "my student government meeting ran long" or "practice let out late" will only create bitterness and frustration as other members try to pick up the pieces. If you value team members, you will value team meetings, and you will make them a priority. Missing a meeting, regardless of the excuse, sends a message that you don't care.

Etiquette might be even more important than logistics when working on a team project. Sometimes team members are so excited and enthusiastic (or so insecure and troubled), they throw good behavior out the window right from the get-go. The most basic, yet toughest to follow 'rule' is that only one person should speak at a time. This guideline should be imposed early on a team. Sure, conversations being what they are, you're going to interrupt and 'step on each other's lines' a bit, but you must agree to hear each other out and truly listen. Here are some tips:

- Everyone has an open notebook, so when ideas and questions surface, they can be jotted down and remembered. This results in less forgetting and less interrupting.

- Before each meeting ends, be sure to clearly state next steps and responsibilities. Ask if anyone has anything else to share and if anyone has any questions or issues. This prevents confusion if anyone needs clarification, and it prevents frustration and hurt feelings due to the perception of not being heard.
- End each meeting with some praise for each other. This includes general praise, like "Nice job, everybody" to individual praise, like "Hey, Jimmy, I'm really digging your idea for a glass gym floor with lines that change depending on the game being played."
- Remind each other often of WITT (We're In This Together)!

2. **Pull your weight.**

   If you pull your weight and give a little extra effort, others are more likely to follow suit, and you'll be on firmer ground if you need to call out any of your teammates for slacking.

3. **Communicate. Communicate. Communicate.**

   With email, texting, video chatting, file-sharing and the like, there's really no excuse for a team's left hand to not know what the right hand is doing. Share early and share often, and keep your mates apprised of your progress.

4. **Agree to a 'Homestretch Rule'**

   At an agreed upon time, as the deadline approaches, the team should shift its emphasis from a PEOPLE focus (i.e. making sure all members are heard and feel valued) to a PROJECT focus (i.e. making sure stuff gets done).

   Of course, dynamics will vary from team to team. Egos may need to be massaged throughout the process for some. For others, your team might have a healthy focus on the project, maturity prevails, and everyone wants what best for the team, regardless of whether their ideas are selected or what roles were assigned.

   For most, a consistent acknowledgement of the value of all members throughout the process is important. More important, arguably, is an acknowledgement that you will not be evaluated on the personal relationships you establish but on the quality of your output, so the importance of the project should be elevated slightly above the importance of the people. Having said this, there is no quicker way to undercut your success than to have interpersonal issues muck up the works. Just watch any episode of *Survivor* or Donald Trump's *The Apprentice*.

5. When you start to BLAME, think of the GAME.

In the end, the team project was probably assigned to achieve these two goals: 1) Learn something new within the discipline you are studying; and 2) Develop team skills like organization, time and personnel management, public speaking and interpersonal communication.

This is why your professor is having you go through the team process. Your professor knows that you are developing these skills along the way, regardless of the project's outcome. This is why it's sort of like a game.

So, if team dynamics break down, if some unforeseen outside force sidetracks your progress, if a member doesn't pull his weight, don't waste time assigning blame. Just focus on the game of cranking out the best project you can, knowing that you gained and grew and garnered important skills through the good, the bad, and the ugly parts of the process. Remember that school is a testing ground, and you'll pass one test by getting through the team process. However, there may be little or no grade attached to that test. The 'game' of getting a good grade will require a quality project/presentation. So, get off the blame and move on to the game.

★★★

ASIDE: In the 2013 NCAA Men's Basketball Tournament, Louisville guard, Kevin Ware, leaped into the air with all his might in an attempt to block an opponent's shot. When he landed, his lower leg snapped, and the bone gruesomely protruded out of his skin. He was in shock (literally), and his teammates were in a different kind of shock. But the TEAM still had more than half of their game left to play. Realizing that one member could no longer contribute, they did not pack it in and go home. They did not waste time crying, "Woe is me (we?)" or feeling sorry for themselves. There was no time for that. The clock was literally ticking. What they did was set about the business of winning the game. Teammates stepped up their game. New players contributed in new ways. The 'project' was successful. They won the game.

★★★

6. Remember: Justice Prevails.

While it's truly hard to tolerate a team member who's not pulling his weight in the short-term, justice will prevail in about five years' time when you are able to exhibit skills you developed on your team project, and your weak teammate is not. Your boss will appreciate you, and his boss will be frustrated by him (if he's landed a job).

Remember that point when you're grinding it out on a student team that's not functioning well. And, remember this: every experience can be a good experience if you grow from it. Sure, that sounds lame, but sometimes what's lame is just what's real and true. And sometimes the truth hurts. If you think that this will be the last time you'll have to work with a difficult person, think again. Try to just 'enjoy' the ride, knowing you're working on your skills all along the way.

Remember the game.

ASSUMING NO ONE CARES EVEN THOUGH THEY DO

The last few pages have focused on the part of our mantra that assumes no one else cares. While this is a good theoretical strategy — a kind of "Be prepared" scout motto or a "Hope for the best but prepare for the worst"

approach — the honest truth is that there are PLENTY of people who will care about you if you let them. They can help you get to where YOU want to be. So, reach out and ask for help. Just remember that, in the end, you and only you, can be in control of your own destiny. Others can open doors for you, but you need to walk in and make things happen. You need to care more about it than anyone else.

And be prepared for how you'll handle bad teammates and that Frisbee guy!

HOW DO I LOOK?

*(aka Keeping Up with the Joneses
on the Yellow Brick Road)*

*"If a man does not keep pace with his companions,
perhaps it is because he hears the beat of a different drummer.
Let him step to the music which he hears,
however measured or far away."*

— HENRY DAVID THOREAU

One of the toughest challenges for any college student is fighting the urge to compare yourself to your peers. Looking to your left and right is a good practice when you're in need of some campus information or informal peer guidance. However, it can be detrimental when charting your own path and you begin worrying about whether you're on pace with your peers. These insidious comparisons are what old people call "Keeping up with the Joneses." It distracts you from your dreams and it can only make you miserable. Steve Jobs suggested as much in a commencement address he gave to Stanford students, telling them:

> *"Your time is limited, so don't waste it living someone else's life. Don't be trapped by dogma—which is living with the results of other people's thinking. Don't let the noise of others' opinions drown out your own inner voice. And most important, have the courage to follow your heart and intuition. They somehow already know what you truly want to become. Everything else is secondary."*

Be forever cognizant that your peers' goals are not yours and their path is not yours. They might have some good ideas and strategies, and you should feel free to adopt what's applicable to your situation. But if you start saying, "Oh look, she's got her career path figured out, but I don't," and you decide to jump into a major just to 'keep pace,' it can have serious repercussions. You will be making hasty decisions based on the wrong reasons. You won't be finding and following your bliss, and you could get sidetracked from your own path. It could cost you credits and tuition dollars, and it could lead to the mid-life misery mentioned in the introduction of this book.

So, remind yourself regularly that throughout your entire life there will always be people who are more, and less, intelligent than you, with greater, and lesser, social skills and physical talents. This is a blessing to avoid boredom! Rather than succumbing to defeatism and self-critique, take inspiration and motivation from those with more than you. And continually seek ways to help those with lesser abilities.

Remember Dorothy and her friends from *The Wizard of Oz?* They might be good models here. (If you can get those images of flying monkeys out of your head, that is!) Scarecrow, Tin Man and the rest were not trying to keep up with the Joneses. They were not in competition, real or imagined, with each other. They were on a parallel journey along that yellow brick road, helping each other reach their own individual goals. Sure, it's simplistic, but it's also quite similar to your college journey. You'll pick up friends along the way, each with distinct goals in mind for the end. You'll encounter challenges, distractions and failures along the way. But if you support each other in your separate, parallel endeavors, you'll get where you need to be.

Fortunately, you won't wake up and realize it's all been a tornado-induced dream. It'll be your life. So listen to your friends and vicariously enjoy their journeys. But when it comes to your own goals, your own journey, keep listening to what Gandhi called 'that still small voice within.'

★★★

(Give me a break. I know some of you are saying, "Dude, this comparison totally breaks down 'cause Dorothy had really hit her head, and even in the dream-state it was the ruby slippers that did all the heavy lifting. Those knuckleheads were lucky to get past the poppy field while I've got serious stuff to deal with at college!" I hear your concerns, and I applaud your critical thinking, but it's just a measly metaphor. Suspend your disbelief and have some fun with it, will ya?!)

Oh yeah. One last point regarding academics: Don't panic! There are a whole lot of idiots who have successfully navigated college and graduated. Moreover, if you believe you are capable, that's half the battle. Or, put differently, 'fake it until you make it.' There is a great *Harry Potter* scene where Dumbledore says, "Once again, I must ask too much of you, Harry." It is a wonderful illustration of how we truly can expect young people to step up and rise to myriad challenges. At times, the demands may seem overwhelming. However, many college students experience the joy of surprising themselves with their resilience and potential, meeting challenges with previously undiscovered strength, and rising to the occasion. You can be one of them.

You'll do fine.

Just don't be so driven that you forget about livin'…which is next.

LIVING:
THE NON-ACADEMIC PART

(aka 'The Game of Life')

"I never let schooling get in the way of my education."
— MARK TWAIN

There's way more to college than book learnin'. There are sporting events, concerts, intramural activities, art shows, theater, political demonstrations, philanthropic endeavors, guest speakers, and every possible club activity under the sun, from *a cappella* singing to rock climbing to Quidditch. (Yes, there are even intercollegiate Quidditch competitions nowadays.)

It's all education. It's a rich panoply of experiences that you may *never* again have within your daily grasp. When you're part of a college community, you're a built-in audience for famous and almost famous people who want to share stuff with you. As a result, "people will come" (to quote that wonderful *Field of Dreams* line - Look it up!). They will come to your campus to share their cool stuff with you. And, although there are myriad enrichment opportunities all around you on a college campus, you need to be ACTIVE and INTENTIONAL about getting the most out of them because, unlike high school, no one will force you to do anything. You can sit passively and watch the world go by rather than being a part of it.

Do yourself a favor: choose to be a part of it!

"I wanted to live deep and suck out all the marrow of life...."

~HENRY DAVID THOREAU

Okay. So, we already saw this quote when we were introducing the *Carpe College!* concept. That's true. But it's a great outlook, so we're repeating it. Yes, Thoreau was talking about living in the woods, and we're talking about moving beyond the books on a college campus, but the idea is the same. If you wish to truly experience the life you're embarking upon, you need to do it deeply. Why? First of all, because you want to have a rich life. It will be more interesting and more exciting, and you'll end up with better stories to tell. Also, the more exploring and experimenting you do, the better chance you have of finding your place in the universe. As mentioned earlier, Joseph Campbell called it "Follow Your Bliss." Others have said things like, "Do what you love, and the money will follow." The ideas are the same. You want to find something to love *and* find a way to spend your life doing that. At eighteen, however, how do you know what you love unless you try lots of stuff? Whatever it turns out to be, it's probably not going to stroll up and tap you on the shoulder. It will require effort and experimentation and experience. Your college campus, with all its great offerings, is the perfect setting for this kind of experimentation and for this kind of experience. It can become your very own laboratory for finding your passion, for finding yourself. It just requires your effort. So, make the most of it.

(If you're one of those fortunate few who's already found what you love, or one

who has had a very active and cosmopolitan high school experience, please be open to the fact that college will offer literally thousands of new academic subjects and extra-curricular experiences that will be new to you. Even if you are happy with your set path, don't miss out on the opportunity to soak in all that new bliss.)

Maybe finding your bliss or your place in the universe seems a bit too lofty at this stage. That's fine. Let's get crass (or practical) and set our sights on finding a job then. It turns out that everything suggested above – all that non-academic stuff – is also wonderful preparation for the practicalities of seeking employment. Of course, every time you plan your week, organize your life, study for a test, conduct research, take notes, work on a team, give a presentation, or think analytically, you are developing and honing important skills that will be marketable in the workforce. They are built into your academic pursuits. HOWEVER, there's important stuff built into your non-academic life as well, and we'll explore that in the coming pages.

But, before we venture into this new terrain, let's remind ourselves once again of our mantra:

"Know Thyself. Have a Plan. Assume No One Else Cares."

Whether it's finding cool campus events, finding yourself socially, or finding a career path that seems right to you, this mantra can be your guide.

"I'M THINKING COLLEGE BUT HE'S TALKING CAREER?!"

(aka Finding Work Will Be...well...work!)

"My so-called career is a haphazard thing."
— PAUL MCCARTNEY

Remember "The June Question" I mentioned before, where I ask my students what they want to be able to say in June following their first year? It's about projecting yourself forward so you can plan in the present. Well, you can ask a similar question as you imagine your life at graduation time, looking out on your future life after college:

What do you want to be able to say at graduation?

Having some good job prospects will probably be on the list of things you'd like to be able to say. So, here's an idea about putting your non-academic life to work for you.

THE JOB OF GETTING A JOB.

When you graduate and interview for a job, regardless of whether you want to be an accountant or an anthropologist, a banker or a biologist, a designer or a DEA agent, the process will all go about the same:

- A job will be posted (more likely, you'll hear of it through word-of-mouth & networking)
- Many candidates will apply

- Through resume reviews and interviews, the large pool will be winnowed down to a couple of finalists
- On paper (and in the interview) these finalists will look NEARLY IDENTICAL!!!

That's right. When it comes down to the cream of the crop, they're going to look about the same. You could almost flip a coin to choose between them. They will have good grades, solid experience with campus organizations, probably a leadership role of some sort, a practical experience through an internship or two, some awards, and the requisite skills (or promise) the employer is looking for. As a result, if we were examining their resumes side by side, it would force us down, down, down the page to begin to differentiate between the two candidates. We'd have to get to the bottom where people list the interesting personal stuff that makes them unique: Eagle Scout, drummer, rodeo clown, cliff jumper, ukulele player.

While these seem like throw-away items, they're actually VERY important. When everything else about the candidates is identical, these 'funkier' elements begin to distinguish one from the other.

So, armed with all this information, the straightforward and the funky, the employer may then invite the final candidates to an interview lunch, where several members of the employer's team will 'break bread' with the candidate. Now, there are plenty of books and advice columns telling you how to manage such a lunch, like avoiding pasta with red sauce or a messy chicken salad sandwich. It's assumed the finalists will have done their homework in this regard and won't make a mess. And it's assumed they will have done their homework on the prospective employer's work and operations, so when the conversations become 'shop talk,' they will have a clue.

HOWEVER, most of the banter around the lunch table will NOT be about the candidate's resume, and it will NOT be about the work at the office. The conversations will be as varied as a Thanksgiving dinner table, spanning diverse topics from movies, the arts, politics, sports, travel, and world news. And, the content of these conversation will be VERY important in the late stages of the hiring process because this will allow the candidates to demonstrate how interesting they are. This will be where 'the team' gets a sense of who 'the person' is and whether or not they can work with him day in and day out. This is where the candidate will tell the story about being a rodeo clown for a summer, what he learned from the experience, and why he chose to do it in the first place. This is where the candidate's character, perspective, passion and approach to life are truly revealed.

Nine times out of ten, after resumes are reviewed and interview lunches are over, the candidate who is the MOST INTERESTING PERSON will be hired. These are the kinds of people employers want on their teams. These are the kinds of people employers want around them on a daily basis. And these are the kinds of people I encourage ALL my college students to become.

Time flies. And, just like high school, your college years will fly by. So, setting about the business of becoming the most interesting person you can be needs to start early, happen often, and be part of a strategic plan that is actually predicated more on fun than anything else. The residual effects, however, will include great preparation for the very serious domain of the job market.

BRING IN DA FUNK!

To become a finalist candidate for your first job out of college, you'll need a track record of performing well, some knowledge of your discipline, and a decent skill set that includes communication and interpersonal skills. However, to beat out the other finalists, you will need to be INTERESTING and PASSIONATE. Passion is one of those intangibles that one acquires organically (by finding your bliss, possibly), so we'll focus on becoming more interesting, which is something you can actually work toward in a strategic and intentional way (as long as it's authentic too).

If your goal is to be a more interesting person, then you simply CANNOT behave the way you've always behaved in your established comfort zone. You'll need to 'funk' things up a bit, try new things, and take some risks.

All of this funkiness can be contained in a simple approach:

Meet interesting people and do interesting stuff.

MEET INTERESTING PEOPLE

Your Peers. When you arrive on a college campus, you are entering a wonderfully diverse community where students come from all walks of life, all parts of the world, with all kinds of interests. They have the potential to make your life VERY interesting, to expand your view of the world as well as your place in it. If you keep your nose glued to your books or your computer screen, if you keep your dorm room door closed, or if you keep your chin planted firmly against your chest with your eyes down when you stroll across campus, you will miss out on the wonderful opportunity to get to know these people. However, if you are just the slightest bit open to meeting other people, something as simple as opening your dorm door, keeping your eyes up, and a bit of idle chit-chat with classmates, you will be introduced to one of the greatest and richest parts of the college experience: other students.

In fact, you will have to work extra hard NOT to interact with these wonderful people. It should happen almost organically. It should seem like just a natural part of life simply because you've been dropped into this unique and rich environment. If you're fortunate, your roommate will be from another part of the country or, better yet, another part of the world, and invite you home for spring break. If you're lucky, and most of you will be, your dorm floor will have people with different cultural and geographic backgrounds. Some will be interested in sports, some in the arts, some in politics, and some with an entrepreneurial flair may tinker around for the next great computer app. All of these folks will pass you on the way to the shower. You don't even need to leave your dorm floor! Now, imagine whom you could meet as you expand the field to the rest of the dorm, to your walk across campus, your classes, and all the other activities? You can really meet a lot of interesting people, and you can become significantly more interesting as a result.

There's really no excuse! So... Door open. Eyes up. Smile on...

Your Professors. That's right. Your professors are interesting people, too! Students often overlook their professors, seeing them as just part of the institutional machinery, there to crank the process along. Similarly, some students see their professors as just another resource, like Wikipedia, to tap into for assistance only when needed if they have some burning question. Otherwise, why even talk to them? But this attitude results in a serious missed opportunity, and I'd like you to consider a totally different approach to experience this rich collection of interesting people.

I recommend a blanket approach, or 'casting a wide net.' During the first three weeks of each term, make a plan to go in and meet each and every one of your professors. Hit 'em all. If you're taking four to five courses each semester, you'll meet eight to ten professors each year with the potential for about 32-40 over your whole college career. That's a lot of interesting people to get to know!

Now, human nature being what it is, it's clear that you're not going to make a great connection with every professor. That's why you 'hit 'em all' in the hope of developing a couple of relationships each year that are solid and you feel good about, relationships where you like and respect that professor, and that professor likes and respects you. Imagine how much more rich and interesting your life will be just by knowing someone like that?

If all this sounds nice but the benefits are a bit fuzzy, try this... Here are some concrete benefits of getting to know your professors:

- You'll feel more at ease with day-to-day interactions, like asking them questions in class or about class.
- They might be working on some interesting research and ask you to help, an experience that would go right onto your resume! (This happened with me but not until my senior year. If I had been more active and intentional, like I'm suggesting you should be, this may have happened sooner and opened up even more opportunities.)
- They might become the perfect person to turn to when you need a letter of recommendation for an internship, fellowship, grad school, or employment.
- They might become a mentor FOR LIFE! Imagine a relationship where you and your professor like each other, have shared interests and regular conversations, and that continues when you leave college to embark on the rest of your life's journey. Your professor will give you advice about career and life choices, and she will turn to you for advice and insight when you're a professional 'out in the field.'

Talk about a symbiotic relationship! Now, imagine that you have more than one of those. How interesting would your life be then?

So, get busy! Here's how to begin to get the ball rolling:

1. Drop in on your professor during office hours (or make an appointment).
2. Spend 15-20 minutes chatting.
3. Say thanks and leave.

It's just that simple. If you're not big on 'chatter,' here's some material:

- Walk in with a specific question about your course material.
- Follow up with a question about how the course might relate to your field of interest. (e.g. "Professor Brainiac, what do you think about the connection between this calculus concept and the kind of work I'll be doing as a civil engineer?")

  Or....

- Walk in and ask your professor about his or her career path because you're looking for insights as you plan your own. They love to talk about themselves (in a good way) and dole out advice (in a good way), so they'll handle the bulk of the conversation from there.

  NOTE: If you're a bit nervous about 'walking in cold,' most schools have faculty bios on their websites, so you can learn a lot about your professors before meeting them.

  Or try this:

- Walk in with the sole purpose of just introducing yourself. If they're not too busy, professors love this! If they are too busy, be flexible and try again later. Either way, your first stop can be a quick five minutes with a quick exit and a good first impression. The conversation might look like this:

YOU: Hi Professor Brainiac. I'm Mark from your Monday afternoon Political Science class (Shaking hands).

PROF: Hi there. Yes, you look familiar. What can I do for you?

YOU: Nothing really. I just wanted to stop by and introduce myself. I'm from Florida, so I'm just trying to get used to my new surroundings here in the northeast, and I wanted to get to know my professors a little bit. If you have time later on this semester, I'd like to chat with you about the voting process. Now that I'm old enough to vote, I've been reading a bit about voter fraud and voter intimidation in the recent election. I'm really fascinated by this and interested in finding some solutions. I'm guessing you'll have some insights.

PROF: Well, you have certainly come to the right place! I'd love to chat more, but I'm swamped right now. Send me an email, and we'll set up some time to meet again. As a matter of fact, one of my grad students is working on some research in this area, and maybe you can tag along with him.

YOU: That sounds great. Will do. Nice to meet you (Shaking hands), and I'll see you in class.

PROF: Nice to meet you, too, Mark. See you then.

See how easy that is?! Here are a couple more things to think about:
- 'Shaking hands' doesn't mean you should be nervous. It means SHAKE HIS HAND!
- Be sure to use your own name. "Mark" would be weird if it's not your name.
- Be sure to follow up! The idea is to establish a good relationship and have the professor remember you fondly, not to remember you as that guy who never followed up when he's deciding whether or not he should bump your 89% up to an 'A'.
- Here's a real-world example... One of my students, we'll call him Kenny, got to know his computer science professor during his first year. That professor asked Kenny to stay for the summer and help out with some research, which Kenny gladly did, and it resulted in a great learning experience. The following year, Kenny applied for a highly-coveted internship with a premier computer software company on the west coast. Kenny drew upon his relationship and research experience with this professor to help him secure the internship, and he headed out to Seattle the following summer. The internship was a wonderful experience. He got a free laptop, enough money to pay for junior year tuition, and an invitation to do another internship with this company the following summer. While Kenny is a bright and hard-working student, cultivating that relationship with his professor played a significant role in all the wonderful opportunities that followed. Making the initial contact with your professors can open several doors, many of which you cannot even begin to predict.

Finally, I hate to insult professors, but there's one more good reason to try to get to know your professors outside of class. There's an old adage professors have been forced to live by: "Publish or Perish." This means they need to publish their research or miss out on rich professional opportunities. (Look it up!) At the classroom level, it *may* mean that they are expected to be better at research and being an expert in their field than they are at being a good teacher. This could mean that you may not be getting their 'best work' in the classroom, or that talking to a group of 200 people does not play to their strengths. So, cultivating a one-on-one relationship with that professor outside of class might give you inroads to a great thinker & teacher, one you may not have gotten to experience in a classroom setting.

Cultivating these relationships with professors will pay off on the practical level (getting questions answered, getting a recommendation letter, etc.), but it will also provide a rich college life for you and make you a more interesting person in the end.

DO INTERESTING STUFF

Bulletin Board Bingo. When I was in college, I fell into a habit that turned out to be an excellent one, and I thank my parents to this day for their contribution to it. Though we didn't have a lot of money, my parents bought me a season pass (and an extra ticket for a friend) to the large auditorium theater on campus that hosted all the big stage productions. This was a very smart move on their part, for I was mostly interested in sports at the time, and there was plenty of that to go around on my Big Ten campus. This theater pass, however, exposed me to the Joffrey Ballet and traveling Broadway shows. There was a David Mamet theater festival, Shakespeare, modern dance, and even some of the tamer, or more intimate, rock concerts that were not designed for the basketball arena (though I went to see those, too). My parents had given me an excuse to make these new experiences part of my college experience, and by opening up those possibilities, I found myself seeking out others as well. I didn't just go to those huge productions. I went to the smaller, more experimental theater productions, too. I went to 'strange' movies. I went to art shows and political speeches and music recitals and guest lectures. If my friends would come with me, we'd go as a group. If not, I'd 'fly solo' and meet new people when I got there.

I still had time for my own intramural sports and the big games on the weekends, but this rich new world was opening up to me, and it was predicated upon doing interesting stuff. Moreover, I decided to try one of these new experiences once a month, and it made for a consistently rich college life.

Later, when I taught high school, I would encourage all my seniors to adopt this habit when they went off to college. That's when I named it "Bulletin Board Bingo" (BBB) and encouraged them to make it a habit in college and the rest of their lives. They, along with my current college students, have been doing it for nearly two decades now, and I'm always thrilled to hear about their great experiences.

Here's how you play *Bulletin Board Bingo:*

1. Put "BBB" in your calendar on the 15th of each month as a reminder. If the 15th rolls around, and you haven't played Bulletin Board Bingo yet, you'll still have two weeks.
2. Find an event that's outside your comfort zone posted on any bulletin board around campus.

(Some campus email systems allow you to receive regular updates on upcoming events, so sign up for that, too. Or, if there's an app, try that. Whatever you do, fight the urge to ignore campus events emails. There will be a LOT of them, and you will become tempted to blow right past them or automatically delete them. PLEASE DON'T! Scan them quickly, and you will periodically strike gold with something that appeals to you or confuses you or angers you or inspires you. These are the ones you want.)

3.   Throw caution to the wind, invite your friends or fly solo, and choose to attend that event.
4.   Become more interesting.

It's that simple. And, many of the cool and intersting things on a college campus are free or really inexpensive for college kids on a tight budget.

Now, not every experience will be a hit. Maybe that's why 'BINGO' is an appropriate name. You don't get a winner every time. If you're going to try new things and expand your horizons, you run the risk that not everything will appeal to you. For example, one of my former students went off to college and emailed me to tell me of a BBB experience. She said she had gone to a play that was a little too 'modern' for her taste. She said that everyone on the entire stage for the entire play was naked. Although this wasn't her cup of tea, she recognized that she had a memorable experience, nonetheless, and she would have a great story to tell down the road. So, she chalked it up to experience and got right back on the BBB horse the following month.

If you make *Bulletin Board Bingo* a habit in your life by doing something interesting each month, you will have accumulated more than 30 new and rich experiences by the time you graduate from college, and you will be a much more interesting person as a result. Then, when you end up in an interview lunch and the conversation moves to any number of topics, you will have plenty of points of entry into that conversation. If you spend your college years myopically attending to only those things related to your major or only those things that feel familiar and safe, never stretching your areas of interest or never taking risks by trying new things, then that could be one VERY quiet interview lunch (and a very quiet life to follow).

One final BBB thought: consider the VALVE company (Look it up!), whose revised employee handbook recently made the online circuit for all to see. This entertainment company has a 'flat' organizational structure, it hires 'great' people, and turns them loose (on their very first day) to make decisions about what projects to work on or, if they don't find any existing projects of value, to create new ones. They give their employees an inordinate amount of freedom to make decisions about how they spend their days and how they'll contribute to the company's well being.

Why do they put such trust in their employees? Because they hire *'T-shaped individuals'* (Look it up!), people who have deep expertise in one area (the vertical part of the 'T') and a moderate amount of ability in several other areas (the horizontal part of the 'T'). These folks have depth and breadth, making them great collaborators (team players) and allowing them to see connections between concepts or disciplines that may not seem connected on the surface. VALVE may have taken their cues from another innovative company, IDEO (Look it up!), who also sees great value in T-individuals.

So, how do you become a T-individual? Play a little Bulletin Board Bingo and continue to be curious about everything.

(We'll cover more about BREADTH a bit later.)

One Final Interesting Note About Becoming More Interesting. Remember that everything you do at college should be predicated on our mantra: "Know Thyself. Have a Plan. Assume No One Else Cares." So, when you consider what 'taking risks' or 'stretching yourself' might look like, it would be wise to reflect first about who you have been and who you'd like to become. Then figure out how much elasticity you'll have in exploring the latter. Of course, you don't have a firm idea yet of who you will become, so that's where the exploration and risk come in. I'd recommend following Rear Admiral Grace Hopper's advice: "It's easier to ask forgiveness than it is to get permission." So, don't spend a lot of time asking the person you've been for permission to try new things. Just do them and forgive yourself later if things don't turn out just right. You'll be amazed how forgiving people can be about 'stuff you tried in college.' As long as you're not harming yourself or others, I say go for it. Just don't post it all on Facebook!

Here's a page of great things my students tried BEFORE they arrived at college:

Climbed a Jamaican waterfall

Performed in Carnegie Hall★

Rebuilt a PS3

Rode a bike off a cliff into a lake★

Started business with sister

Sang at Pearl Harbor anniversary in Hawaii

Developed curriculum & worked at LGBTQ youth center★

Skied shirtless (FYI, submitted by a GUY!)

Renovated basement into a bar

Went to First Robotics Championship in St. Louis

Jumped off a cliff on snowboard

Interned at Norton Museum of Art★

Drafted a policy that 14 school districts adopted★

Welded a sculpture

Flew a Cessna plane in Alaska

Qualified for nationals in 3 diving events★

Got a motorcycle license

Went skydiving

Watched 4th of July fireworks over Niagra Falls from hot air balloon

Explored abandoned buildings★

Built trebuchet out of friend's deck★

Spent 3 weeks on Guatemala service trip★

Went backstage @ broadway musical

Blew up a car's airbag

Petted a squirrel★

Swam with sharks

Wrote 80-pg autobiography & 1st person video game from scratch★

Finished a triathlon★

Wrote a novel★

Slept in 37 different places on high school campus★

Went to China alone

Built Linux from scratch★

Did wing-suit gliding

Built a firewall★

Fought a bear

Went on tour w/favorite band

Was globally recognized for work★

Saw Northern Lights in Alaska

visited Morocco

Talked to space station crew via live uplink★

Touched Taylor Swift (Not to be confused with previous 'petted a squirrel')

THAT WAS A GREAT START. IMAGINE WHAT THEY DID ONCE THEY GOT TO COLLEGE!!

Okay. One MORE Final Interesting Note About Becoming More Interesting. A wise somebody somewhere once said, "If you have a free weekend, you're not doing it right." Any college experience offers enough on the academic, social and personal development fronts that a free weekend means you're definitely not carpe-ing enough.

★ While many on the list cost money, these activities were done for little or no cost!

KEEP YOUR EYES ON THE CAREER PRIZE

"...their graduations hang on the wall,
but they never really helped them at all.
No, they never taught them what was real...."

— BILLY JOEL

With all of this Hippie talk about finding yourself and taking risks and soaking up all the wonderful stuff outside of class, it's important to realize that part of *Carpe College!* is also about gaining some perspective for what comes AFTER college. And, as much as we may not want to admit it, a job (or if we might be so bold, a career) should be a part of that plan. Whether you have a distinct idea of what you'd like to be when you grow up, or you haven't a clue, the first year of college is a great time to BEGIN to ratchet up your career exploration.

So, in addition to becoming a more interesting person (which will be great for your job interviews and for life), you also need to use your college years to gain perspective about potential career opportunities, to actually do a bit of career exploration homework.

There are a few lucky ones among you who know EXACTLY what you want to do with your lives. If the three of you would please take a seat against the wall, I'd like to chat with everyone else for a moment....

There may have been a lot of chatter and lip service ever since middle school about finding your career path. Maybe your teachers administered some career interest inventories or a Myers-Briggs Personality test, or maybe there was even some career-focused curriculum. And, although many of you were asked to make some sort of decision related to selecting a major or a path of study for your college, it's likely that there still may be some pangs of uncertainty.

That's fine and natural and, given the lack of exploration freedom you Millennials have been granted, it's totally understandable. So, let those pangs pang away!! And don't panic.

Know thyself. Have a plan. Assume no one else cares.

After you've reminded yourself of our mantra, take a peek at this strategic plan for beginning the next phase of your career search. It's a plan that's relatively painless, takes little effort, and can be launched before your first winter break!

THE CARPE CAREER! PLAN

The List

Between now and winter break, create a list of professional people ('experts') you know in your field of interest, who might be able to provide some insights about careers. If you're interested in biology, but uncertain about which biological field to explore, cast a wide net. Do you have an uncle who's a biology professor? An aunt who's a doctor? What about the veterinarian you've been taking your dog to for years? Are you on good terms with your high school biology teacher? What about that guest speaker from the local zoo? Wasn't there a kid on your football team whose mom was a forensic scientist with the police department? All of these are great people to put on your 'expert' list. What if you're interested in a very esoteric field, like computer game design, and you don't know anyone who knows anyone who does that? Well, have you read any gaming magazines that mention the gaming gurus who are taking that world by storm? Throw those guys' names on your expert list! It certainly can't hurt.

What if you have absolutely no idea about anyone in your field of interest? What a great excuse to pop in and see your professors. Ask them if they have any names. Many professors have contacts all over the planet. (Good thing you've been cultivating all those great relationships with your profs!!) Your campus career center probably has an alumni network you can tap into, as well, and there's nothing wrong with venturing online to see some cool *TED Talks* and contacting some of those 'famous' people.

The Letter

Well, we know letters have gone the way of the cassette tape, so let's just make it an email. Draft an email to everyone on your list (the more difficultly famous folks might take some resourcefulness to track down their addresses). This email should be short and sweet and to the point. You're a student looking for some guidance. You can follow or modify the template in this box as you see fit.

If you're concerned about sending a 'cold call' letter out of the blue, don't be. Most people would love an opportunity to help out a young student, and you've just given them the opportunity. There will be few other times in your life when you can play a card like 'the student card,' so use it while you can. Most professional people will respond with a kind note when they find a moment to breathe. If you don't get a response, maybe you got lost in their spam filter. If they're high on your list of important people, then try again in about a month. Don't guilt-trip them. Just follow up. After that, if they still don't respond, just make a new list: "People I'll be sure to fire when

> Subject: Student Seeking Advice
>
> Dear Ms. Wisenheimer:
>
> I am a first-year student at Clueless U. who is interested in (insert your career aspirations here) and looking for some guidance. I'm good at (insert some stuff you're good at) and I'm especially interested in (insert stuff you like, general career ideas, or courses you like here), but I don't have a good sense of how this might translate into career opportunities. If you would be so kind as to answer a few of these questions to the best of your ability, I would truly appreciate it.
>
> * How did you prepare for your career?
> * How did you break into it?
> * What do you love about it?
> * What do you hate about it?
> * How do you spend most of your days?
>
> I thank you, in advance, for any responses or additional advice you can provide.
>
> Sincerely,
>
> K. Reer Hunter

I become king of the world." Just kidding. Assume they're on an extended vacation or simply not interested and don't waste any more mental energy wondering about it. Of course, be sure to check YOUR OWN spam filter to ensure that their response is not sitting in YOUR email box.

The Leap (aka The Bait and Switch or "You want more?!")

After you've received a nice response from the nice professional person, it's time to ask for more.

(Oooops. First read their note and be sure it was a NICE note.)

Now, despite the seemingly negative header of this section about wanting more or 'baiting and switching,' asking for more falls into the categories of 'it can't hurt to ask,' 'what's the worst that can happen?' and 'if you don't ask, you'll never know.' Remember, you're playing your student card, so ask, ask, ask!

Ask for what? The biggie! An opportunity to 'shadow' this professional person for a day at their job. This email should sound something like the letter shown in the box.

Dear Ms. Wisenheimer:

Thank you so much for your generous response and thoughtful note. Your insights will serve me well as I continue to explore who I am, what might be out there for me, and how I might contribute to a better world.

If I may be so bold, I was wondering if you would ever entertain the idea of allowing me to 'shadow' you at your job for a day, either during my winter or summer break. I'm hoping such an observational experience will give me heightened perspective on the field of (insert field here) and a taste of 'the real world'.

If you think it would be feasible, please let me know.

Again, thank you so much for your helpful response.

Sincerely,

I. M. Needy

Of course, planning and logistics are going to come into play both before and after you make such a request. If you live in Ohio and Ms. Wisenheimer lives in California, this will be tougher (and more expensive). So, start with people geographically close. If you live in Cleveland, and your uncle works there, start with him. I'd recommend that a 2-hour driving radius from your home would be reasonable. That's a long drive, and it will be a long day, but it's an investment you should be willing to make. Let's put it in perspective... Take the longest road trip you've made for fun with your friends, cut it in half, and make that your geographic radius.

Now, let's consider some tougher scenarios. Let's say that you're looking at becoming a computer game designer, and all those people are on the coasts while you're stuck in the 'flyover' states. (As a Midwestern kid, I've always hated that term.) Jack B. Nimble, the hottest game designer on the planet actually responded to your email, and you want to spend a day with him. What to do?! You're going to have to get creative and you're going to have to look at your budget. Here are some options:

- Ask Jack if they have an office near your home in Ohio.
- Ask Jack if he knows of other game designers closer to your home.
- Talk to your folks about a potential family trip to California, so you can see Jack.
- Do you have any relatives you can visit near Jack?

- Do you have any friends who want to road trip to Jack-ville?
- Tell Jack that it's a long way and very cost prohibitive, and ask if he'd be willing to create a mini-internship that covers the costs of your travel and lodging if you made the trip. (I said you might have to get creative! In fact, now would be a great time to send Jack some of your cool ideas or projects you've worked on to make him 'hungrier' to meet you.)

All of this is really as simple as it sounds (depending upon geography of course): The List. The Letter. The Leap. It's just that simple.

Here are some supplemental tips:

- Try one shadowing experience during your first winter break. This allows you to get used to it, and it demonstrates to yourself, and to others, that you're serious about your future. Then do 3-4 shadow experiences over your next summer break and continue to pepper your college breaks with similar experiences.
- Every time you shadow someone, ask for another professional's name. This will make the process self-perpetuating and less of a grind. You just set the wheels in motion during your first year and then simply make new contacts and set up shadowing appointments after that.
- Offer to pay for lunch in appreciation for your host's time. They will rarely take you up on it, but be ready with $100 cash in your pocket. When you get home, you can put it right back in your bank, but... Scout's Motto: Be Prepared.
- Treat each experience as a potential first contact for an internship or a 'real job' after college. This is not fantasy. This is REALLY how initial contacts are made.
- Get a decent, professional-looking notebook, take it with you, and jot down ANYTHING you think is interesting: big ideas, names of people you meet, job-related information, questions that emerge. Write down (or record in a voice memo on your phone) everything you remember immediately after. Don't wait until after the long drive home, or you're sure to forget some good stuff.
- Do some homework ahead of time about the person you're visiting and the organization.
- Get your host's business card and write a HAND-WRITTEN thank you note when you get home (or make it an email if they seem too busy for such 'old school' charm).

Remember, the rationale behind all of this is to have a long-term focus designed to give you perspective for the next big decision you'll make in your life – your life after college. That's right. This is about having a plan AND asking forward-thinking questions like, "What do I want to be able to say at graduation time?" Aside from your academic success, you'd probably like to say that you have SOME idea about where you'll turn to next.

Consider this: What if you have decent grades, the economy is decent, and you end up with four job offers coming out of college? How can you possibly choose among those offers if you have no perspective? Well, this approach will help you garner perspective.

Think about it. By graduation time, if you do two big internships, which will give you a relatively 'deep' experience in your field of interest, and you dip your toes in lots of different waters by shadowing many professionals for a day at a time, you will have secured plenty of perspective about how you'd like to proceed. You will have amassed multiple and varied experiences from every professional you visited. Each one will have become a contact and maybe even an advisor, whose counsel you could seek as you make your first career decisions. When it comes time to choose between job offer A or job offer B, you can draw upon all these experiences. Maybe you shadowed someone and thought, "Oh my gosh, they do that 350 days a year. There's not a chance I want to live that way!" On the other hand, maybe you shadowed someone whose job wasn't even really on your radar, but your uncle suggested you check it out, and you walked away from that day saying, "I could *really* see myself doing that day in and day out."

Again, what you are seeking from these professional interactions is *perspective*. Start during your first year and take it slow. Enjoy the experiences and learn from them. It's like a 4-year scavenger hunt helping you make wise decisions about the direction you'll take somewhere down the road. You'll make lots of stops, meeting helpful people along the way, and by the end you'll have a nice collection of goodies. So, plan to experience these professional interactions beginning early in, and peppered throughout, your college career. If you wait until junior or senior year, it will become a chore. You will be stressed, it will be one more thing you HAVE to do, and you won't enjoy it.

Don't do that to yourself. Start soon!

EXPLORE GALORE!

(aka Try Anything)

"I've missed more than 9000 shots in my career. I've lost almost 300 games. Twenty-six times I have been trusted to take the last second shot and missed. I have failed over and over and over again in my life. And that is why I succeed."

— MICHAEL JORDAN, NBA SUPERSTAR

College is a wonderful time of experimentation and discovery. You should push those limits and embrace those opportunities! It's important to remember, however, that YOU WILL MAKE MISTAKES!! ALL THE GREAT ONES DO!!

While such experimentation is designed to encourage you to push your own limits, stretch your boundaries, test new waters and broaden your horizons, of course, you'll need to conduct yourself under the guiding principles of our mantra again:

Know thyself. Have a plan. Assume no on else cares.

This is YOUR life, after all, and only you can determine where to draw the line between exploration and recklessness. The key here is to push yourself while following the medical profession's Hippocratic oath: Do No Harm. Of course, this begs further questions about what constitutes 'harm.' One might wonder, 'How can I push the limits and make mistakes without causing any harm? Don't I create harm simply by making any mistake?'

Well, sure. But save that for Philosophy class!

Mistakes are, by their very nature, harmful (to varying degrees). Smaller mistakes result in short-term, short-lived harm, and that leads us to one more mantra: "No Pain. No Gain." You'll need to experiment a bit, suffer through the mistakes a bit, and emerge better and stronger as a result.

So, proceed with some (but not too much) caution. Plan to push yourself, creating a bit of self-inflicted pain (but not too much) in the process. Be determined to limit the 'pain' you cause others in the process, and you will gain in the end.

Those who succeed are those who own their mistakes, learn, grow, and move on. I categorize the *Carpe College!* mistake areas as...

1. Academic – the stuff you'll screw up regarding your studies
2. Social – the stuff you'll screw up in your interactions with others
3. Cultural – the stuff you'll screw up due to a lack of cultural awareness

A great process for handling, and learning from, such mistakes is F^3:

FIX IT – FORGIVE YOURSELF – FORGE AHEAD

Academic Screw Up: Let's say you got to college, found too much freedom, didn't plan well, and failed your first midterm. Then what?

- **Fix it** by managing time better and getting more serious and systematic. Visit your professor to do a 'post-mortem' about what went wrong and to get suggestions about how to proceed. Plan time better by leaving SPECIFIC time each week for that course. Use that time to review (or rewrite) notes from class, to preview what's coming, and to talk to peers in a study group about the material.

- **Forgive yourself** by recognizing that you're in a significant transition in your life, a completely new setting with new 'rules.' It's understandable that it might take some time to get used to. However, repeated 'screw ups' should not get similar forgiveness.

- **Forge ahead** by recognizing that what's next is what matters. If you've fixed things by developing a more systematic plan with a more diligent approach, and you've cut yourself a break, then you can keep your eyes on the prize of successfully completing your first year (short term) and attaining academic success over the long haul.

Social Screw Up: Let's say you got to college and your inexperience with alcohol took center stage. At a Friday party you got sloppy drunk, your roommate had to usher you home early, and you were belligerent and rude to your other dorm mates once you got back to your floor. Of course, you don't remember any of this, but you learn all about it from your dorm pals on Saturday afternoon. Some engage in light-hearted kidding, but some seem a bit more disgusted with you.

- **Fix it** by asking to hear all the gory details and apologizing individually as warranted. Also, throw an impromptu pizza party in the dorm lounge Saturday night as a public apology. Call it the 'I'm Sorry Soiree,' put up a few posters on your dorm floor, order up the food, and say you're sorry one more time when everyone arrives to feed on your free food. Then, consider staying in for the evening. Or, better yet, go out with the gang and stay sober – a great demonstration of your sincerity.

- **Forgive yourself** by recognizing that you're not the first person to have beer bubbles on the brain and have it affect your behavior. You're only human. It can happen, of course, but it's the way you respond that counts. Successive recurrences will make it tougher each time to forgive yourself in the future, so keep that in mind. (It will also be much tougher for others to forgive you, and it will shape their perceptions of you.)

- **Forge ahead** by reflecting on what went wrong and how to prevent it in the future. If you continue to drink socially, find your limits, or don't even tempt your limits. Find a friend who can look out for you, and vice versa. Find an alternative to drinking. Imagine what your outward behavior will look like from an adult's perspective (or in a Facebook photo).

As a bonus, here's another social screw up scenario... Back in college, one of the authors of this book was preparing to embark on a spring break trip to Florida where guys and girls would be staying in hotel rooms together; however, they were truly just friends, and there were no plans for 'hanky panky' (Retro-Lingo-Alert!!). The week prior, one of the girls had her father visit the dorms, and this young college lad (and future author) thought it would be funny when introduced to her father to exclaim, "I will be sleeping with your daughter on this trip." The father showed tremendous restraint, his daughter was frustrated with Idiot Boy, and Idiot Boy learned a great social lesson: don't say everything that comes into your head. It was CLEARLY a social screw up. (Wait... You mean there's only one author of this book?! Hmmm... I guess that Idiot Boy must have been me, then. Ooops.)

Cultural Screw Up: Let's say you get to college, and you begin to realize how limited your upbringing truly was. You encounter Jewish people wearing yarmulkes, Islamic people fasting for Ramadan, African American fraternities hosting 'step shows,' and people putting ketchup on Chicago hot dogs (a real no-no). It's a wonderful new world, but it will highlight how little you may know about other cultures and how much there is to learn. Then there will be the smaller stuff, like misspeaking and saying 'for all intensive purposes,' mispronouncing 'epitome,' having your roommate point out that you're not really a libertarian, or not knowing who Quentin Tarantino is when everyone's discussing their favorite films.

None of this is really a 'screw up.' It's simply a gap in your understanding of the world, and it's perfectly understandable. There's way too much to know, and no one can be expected to learn it all in less than a couple of decades. It's also one of those wonderful parts of being in college, an opportunity to learn outside the classroom, and it will probably happen weekly.

- **Fix it** by making a note of what you didn't understand. Jot it down in your planner or type it into your phone and research it later. Informally, I call this "Filling the Gaps" in my understanding, and it's ongoing.
- **Forgive yourself** by recognizing that there's a reason it's called 'life-long learning' and college is all about opening your eyes to new things. You can't possibly have encountered all of this stuff in your short life. So relax and have fun with it.
- **Forge ahead** by recognizing that EVERYTHING you learn in this fashion will come in handy in the end. Start a list, look stuff up, ask around, and set about the business of accumulating all these wonderful new insights.

A final thought on F³... There's an old adage: 'Fool me once, shame on you. Fool me twice, shame on me.' Most people will give you a second chance when you screw up, but if you don't FIX IT, and you continue in the same way, they won't have the same patience in the future. As long as you're engaged in genuine attempts to make yourself a better person and to continue to grow, most people will be super cool with you.

Okay, just one more final thought on F³... Just as you would like others to forgive you for your missteps, you may wish to consider treating others similarly. A little bit of the 'Do unto others' Golden Rule should apply in your interactions with others during this extremely challenging year. Here's why.... EVERYONE you encounter will be flawed, fallible and simply trying to find their way. For some, they will be meek and quiet. For some, they will act out and flex their muscles - intellectual or otherwise. Some will 'try too hard' and overstep social boundaries. If we can all recognize that we're all in this together, all flawed and fallible and trying to find our way, then more tolerance might be in order. Try to find the right balance between this outlook and the 'fool me once' approach, and you'll end up in a pretty good place.

BE CAREFUL WITH CONTEMPT

In the end, be careful of contempt. If you hold disdain for others more than once per month, you may need to rethink your whole outlook. A perspective in which you look down on others in uber-critical judgment can have a painful way of circling back around and hurting you in the end. It's a lot like karma. Try to give people a break, to find the good in others, to give them a wide berth during their first year of college, this very challenging transitional time when *everyone* is trying to find themselves, and they will do the same for you. If you ever find yourself viewing someone as 'clueless,' try to remember a time when you may have felt embarrassed, and recall that it's not a great feeling. Ask yourself, "Am I simply being a good critical thinker, or am I being contemptuous of others?" If you're leaning toward the latter, try to adjust your outlook, or you may never be able to *Carpe College!*

A CRAZY CONCLUSION

I'd like to close this section with one of my favorite passages from literature. In Ken Kesey's *One Flew Over the Cuckoo's Nest,* the protagonist Randle Patrick McMurphy bets his friends that he can lift a heavy shower room control panel. They all gather in the shower room, he grabs hold of the machine and makes a valiant effort to lift it, but he fails...miserably. The key here is that he knew he couldn't do it even before he tried, but he was trying to encourage the rest of them to get out of their comfort zones and push themselves to take some risk. After the wagered money changes hands and MacMurphy walks away seemingly defeated, he exclaims, "But I tried, though?...I sure as hell did that much, now, didn't I?"

It's a lesson that becomes a turning point in the novel, and it's a GREAT lesson for anyone. Fear of failure is the enemy of *Carpe College!*

Be courageous and be forgiving.

Get out there and TRY!

Ebb & Flow:
Turning Inward & Outward

(Like your belly-button!)

INTRODUCTION

The "Ebb & Flow" section that follows is a collection of wonderful wisdom that's tough to easily categorize. It runs the gamut from lofty philosophical reflection to life in the dorms, from laundry room etiquette to late night parties, from finding your freedom to your new family relationships. All of this stuff involves you, how you think about yourself, and how you relate to the world. So, each chapter will either be about you looking inward (ebb) or you relating outward (flow). These ebbs and flows are not neatly organized, and they don't wash in and out gracefully like the waves on the beach. They're just tossed in here somewhat randomly. If you can't figure out which is which, who cares?! As long as you're looking at yourself as a person who needs to think and live both inwardly and outwardly, you'll be in a great position to *Carpe College!*

Enjoy the ebb & flow that follows…..

FINESSING
YOUR FREEDOM

"Freedom is never voluntarily granted by the oppressor;
it must be demanded by the oppressed."

— MARTIN LUTHER KING, JR.

W hen I was teaching high school seniors, I'd hear the same refrain
from students in the springtime as prom and graduation approached.
They'd complain about their parents constricting their curfew, asking them
where they'd been, or cajoling them to stay home – a renewed tightening of
the reins after students got used to them progressively loosening over their
high school years. It created confusion, consternation and contempt.

As the students and I chatted and drilled deep on this matter, I suggested
what was at the heart of the matter was that their parents were beginning to
feel them slip away. And, with college looming on the horizon, their parents
were simply, and mostly subconsciously, holding on tighter. So, I suggested
an experiment: "Why not promise your parents one full day of YOU? Give
them one day when they can have you all to themselves, you can do whatever they choose with a smile on your face and a spirit of togetherness, and
there will be no questions asked."

There were some gargantuan groans at this suggestion. But many were
desperate and defeated and willing to try anything. (Just the way we teachers
like our seniors!) So some did.

The experiment worked! For the rest of the spring, those who tried
it were beaming about how effective it was, and how it loosened the reins
again. And, they felt pretty strongly that it enhanced their relationship with
their parents when they had serious concerns about it eroding at such an
inopportune time. It secured for them some much needed freedom and

autonomy without damaging this important relationship with people they truly did care about (but were just sick of). Familiarity had bred contempt, and all that jazz. But it didn't have to be lasting.

So, it appears this single sacrifice can land you some much relished freedom if you play your cards right. Give your parents the gift of 'one day of YOU,' and you will be rewarded sevenfold (ish).

NOTE: Since you may not have had your hands on this book in the springtime, I'd recommend 'bookending' your summer with one day of YOU for your folks to start your summer and another at the end, right before you head off to school. You will all feel better for it (If you're a parent reading this before you pass it off to your new high school grad, be sure to let them think this was THEIR idea).

This process will also come in handy during your first breaks at home. It could happen at Thanksgiving, but it will most likely happen at Christmas/ Winter break. You will want to be out at all hours with your friends. Your parents will want to catch up on everything they've missed in your life over the past few months. You will be used to all kinds of newfound freedoms, and your parents will be used to 'their house, their rules.' You will stroll in at 3am, and they will not be happy. Tensions will mount.

You can avoid all of this by judiciously giving them another 'day of YOU' to get 'em off your back (or to rekindle your relationship if you're a parent reading this). It truly will help bring you closer, and it will give you the space and independence you crave. Then, at the end of the break, it'll make letting go that much easier. (Yeah. Kind of like when you try to flick a sticky booger from your finger! Wait... Did I just call you a booger?!)

Baseball great, Willie Stargell, once shared something very obtuse, yet very wise, when he said, "The trick to hitting a baseball is to try easier." Hitting a baseball is one of the toughest things to do in all of sports. The best of the best fail nearly seven times out of ten! I think relationships between parents and their college students can be just as difficult. So, let's do everyone a favor and TRY EASIER!

DO NO HARM

(aka Let's Play Doctor)

As mentioned earlier, "To abstain from doing harm," is an important part of the Hippocratic Oath that all doctors take, and it is a fundamental driver in medical ethics. Of course, it's complicated and not perfect. You might think that sticking a needle in your arm, taking a healthy person's kidney for a transplant, or performing a breast implant can be seen as harmful. However, with these academic nuances aside, the idea behind doing no harm might be a good one to consider for young adults heading off to college. Your 'adult' decisions will help dictate who you are and who you become. With nearly every step you will have the option of doing good or doing harm – to others and to yourself. And, to complicate matters even more, if you choose to do nothing, you will probably still be doing either one or the other.

This book is not a book on ethics, though. It is a book that reminds you to

Know thyself. Have a plan. Assume no one else cares.

In this section of the book, you're going to encounter chapters that span from living in residence halls, where you share a room and cooking and laundry facilities with other people, to your social life, where you'll establish new relationships and probably encounter that difficult terrain of parties, alcohol, drugs and sex. Most of you have navigated this terrain in high school, but few of you have experienced it away from home and out on your own. So, it might be wise to consider who you want to be and how you want to behave when it is YOU ALONE making decisions in this new environment.

I'm reminded of a saying that old, parent-type people like to toss around, and it goes like this: 'Nothing good happens after midnight.' Well, I'm sure there are a whole lot of young people who will disagree with this claim (as well as a couple of older guys like J.J. Cale and Eric Clapton). But there must be some merit to the saying given that it has survived and is oft repeated. Most college parties go well past midnight, many will serve alcohol, and much of the trouble on college campuses is alcohol fueled. So, although it's just an old adage, it appears to contain real wisdom, and it lays some context for the day-in and day-out decisions young college students encounter.

Disney films have such wonderful lessons too (duh!), but sometimes their wisdom comes at you like a bee buzzing past your ear, an encounter with a cute little creature you didn't realize could cause such fright. It happens quickly, it's startling, and it's easy to forget once the initial scare has passed. One of my favorite Disney-wisdom moments occurs in *The Lion King* when Rafiki, the baboon shaman, tells Simba, "You don't even know who you are!" He then delivers him to a reflecting pool where Simba hears the sprit of his father tell him, "Remember who you are" (In that great James Earl Jones voice, of course). Sure, it's a cute, animated adventure, but any young college kid can put him or herself in Simba's shoes (paws?) and find something to ponder.

At college you will have opportunities to cheat and lie and love, to hurt and fight and harm, to dabble in drinking and drugs, to celebrate and copulate, to argue and fight and make peace, to instigate and retaliate, to attack, to abstain, to help, to hinder, to share, to care. Each and every step will pose possibilities, and you will be faced with ethical choices. Even though our mantra challenges you to 'know thyself,' everyone understands that you're still a Simba who can't completely know who you are. But the benefit for you will come from thinking about these lofty things and by asking yourself, "Who am I, where am I going, why and how?" Your answers should guide your behaviors.

The attempt to know yourself, to discover who you are, is what's important. If you're asking the right questions about yourself and reflecting on your behavior regularly, then you're well on your way.

WEEK 1 WISDOM

(Stuff that doesn't often make the list)

"I celebrate myself and sing myself...
I too am not a bit tamed, I too am untranslatable,
I sound my barbaric yawp over the roofs of the world."
— WALT WHITMAN, *SONG OF MYSELF*

When you head off to school, you will probably have a list (or two or three) of stuff you need to bring with you, like lamps, laptops and lip balm. You will have planned well enough to handle your hygiene and hair, tallied up your toiletries to get you through the first term, and secured several new notebooks to get you situated in your first round of classes. However, there's one more thing you may want to consider for your list: The New You.

THE NEW YOU

Are there any alterations or adjustments you'd like to make to that high school kid you used to be? Has anything been gnawing at you regarding your high school days, maybe a nickname or hairstyle or undeserved reputation you've been looking to shed? Any habits you'd like to break (or begin)? Anything you'd like to modify just a bit? If you've had any ideas about remaking or reinventing yourself, NOW is the time to do it. This can take many forms, from the slight to the significant. Here are some authentic examples I've seen:

- Becky wanted to be Rebecca (college is a GREAT place for a name change)
- John, an athlete, wanted to try drama and singing

- Rob, a math guy, wanted to dabble in poetry
- Sarah planned to get more active by running for student government office
- Luke, a 'meat and potatoes' guy, wanted to experiment with veganism
- Sue wanted to simply 'be more outgoing'
- Eric, a great 'book' student, wanted to 'make something with my hands!'

These are all great examples of being intentional about crafting yourself for the next chapter in your life. By the way, if you're completely happy with who you currently are, then by all means, keep doing what you're doing. Either way, if you're reinventing yourself or sticking with your 'status quo' self, plan to reflect at least a little bit on the person you would like to present to your new college community.

When you step onto that campus, of course you'll want to 'be yourself.' But there's nothing that says it can't be a new and improved 'yourself.'

FEET FIRST

I've encountered far too many students who have admirable intentions of focusing on their academic priorities and getting solid footing before jumping into any non-academic activities. Good theory. Bad practice!

You should get your school life in order, of course. Make it a priority. Have a plan, an EMO, etc., etc. -- all that good stuff. But you should also plan to jump into at least one activity feet first. Take a peek at the list of clubs and activities and find something to say YES to. When your RA lopes down the hall trying to recruit for intramural Ultimate Frisbee or the floor social committee, say YES. If there's a table in the student union advertising for Habitat for Humanity or anything else that intrigues you, get involved. Here is one case where it's wiser not to think, but to do. Leap before you look (sort of).

If you're going to *Carpe College!*, you'll need to have these kinds of experiences on your docket. My experience is that those who wait have a tougher time pulling the trigger later. It is far easier to get involved at the outset and bail if school work gets too tough, than it is to hesitate, wait until the time is right, and then try to jump on that moving train. I've seen too many students never find the right time and end up regretting it.

The first week in the dorms is an important one. Much of the social scene and activity is forged during this time. Choose to be a part of it.

Take a Week One Plunge. Carpe! Carpe! Jump into the fray!

DOORSTOPS &
CHOPSTICKS

*"You never really understand a person
until you consider things from his point of view –
until you climb into his skin and walk around in it."*

— ATTICUS FINCH, IN HARPER LEE'S *TO KILL A MOCKINGBIRD*

Hmmmm... What a weird chapter title. What is it? A Jeopardy category? The last two items on somebody's scavenger hunt list? That store at the mall that went out of business after two weeks?

No. It's two things that ought to make their way to the top of your 'school supplies' list.

Huh?!

Well, they're not 'supplies' so much, but they represent two very important elements for your first year, and they can set the tone for your college experience.

DOORSTOPS

Aside from doing well in your classes, keeping your dorm door open may
be the most important thing you do during your first year. (Of course, this
means keeping it open while you're IN your room, and not sleeping or
changing clothes.) Whether you buy one at the store or use a brick, a rock,
or your ugly ceramics project from art class, you need a doorstop. Whatever
you do, KEEP YOUR DOOR OPEN FOR THE FIRST MONTH!

Why?

Because it's the best way to meet new people. And meeting new people
expands your horizons. And expanding your horizons is what *Carpe College!*
is all about. Each new person you meet presents a new opportunity for you
to gain a friend, a study partner, a new member for your club, a teammate
for your intramural volleyball team, or even a future spouse (life partner?).
If your door is shut, you're shutting those people out. Or, at the very least,
you're making it much harder to meet them. Every person who walks by
your closed dorm room door is a missed opportunity. The closed door says
to them, "I'm not interested in getting to know you." If your door is open,
you're saying, "Come on in!" You're essentially telling your dorm mates,
"Hey, I'm open to meeting new people" and "Sure, I'd like you to invite me
to dinner."

It's a subtle signal, but it works!

"But what if I'm studying, and I need quiet?" you might ask. Great
question! And for this I'm going to answer your question with a question:
What if you did your studying somewhere else and reserved your dorm
room for fun, frivolity and fraternizing with your dorm mates? The answer
is that you will probably do better at BOTH studying and socializing. Go
to the quiet floor of the library from 7-10pm, then come back to your room
and fling that door open ready to have some fun. Better yet, you could hang
out in the hallway and create even more social opportunities. Let's put it
this way: if someone's juggling piranhas or debating the second amendment
in the hallway, you're going to want your door to be open, so you don't miss
it.

Moreover, this might be an especially wise approach if you're a more
introverted, shy or reserved person. You could try to become more outgoing with this little step of opening your door (and yourself) to others. And,
it's important to note, the beginning of the school year is the BEST time
to do this because EVERYONE is new, and everyone is in the same boat
where they're trying to meet new people. So, maybe for the first time in a
long time, the shy and reserved person is on the same social plane (or at least

the same starting line) as the more outgoing. Since everyone is new, it's an excellent time to jump right into the social fray as 'equals.'

Consider the alternative: keeping your door closed for the first month while everyone else is establishing social ties, and then, once you've pondered long and hard and finally mustered up the courage, trying to ignite those social connections several weeks later. This is clearly a MUCH tougher proposition. You'll feel like you're running in mud and can't catch up.

Make it easy on yourself, and others, with the simple 'open door' maneuver.

HINT: In the end, this is not really about doors, but about you. OPEN or CLOSED? That is the question.

★★★

(NOTE: Another good reason for an 'open door' policy is that you will be less susceptible to some of the old-school dorm pranks I witnessed. One particularly mean prank involved filling an old record album jacket or large envelope with baby powder, sliding the open end under someone's dorm door and jumping on it. When the dust settled, so to speak, the entire room and its inhabitants were caked in white dust. It's a short-lived laugh for everyone but the victims, and with all the electronic devices lying around in dorm rooms today, this act is sure to result in punches thrown, reports filed, or money exchanging hands to replace damaged computers and phones.

Another, less destructive, prank was to 'penny' people in their dorm rooms. While a room was occupied with the door closed, someone would wedge a stack of pennies, one-by-one, between the door and its jamb near the door lock. As the stack of pennies increased, it put immense pressure on the door latch, essentially rendering it immobile, stuck tight, along with the room's inhabitants. They were 'pennied in.' Of course, this could become quite destructive if the perps fled the scene and there was a fire alarm or similar emergency. That could have been ugly.

See.... If you don't wish to fall victim to these terrible pranks, practice the open door policy. You'll never get 'pennied in' or get a baby powder blast!)

CHOPSTICKS

Okay, so you may be wondering how chopsticks are related to doorstops. The answer is simple. They're both about expanding your horizons. In addition to meeting new people, college is a great place to learn new things (duh!). But many of these new things can be based in community and culture, as well as in the classroom, and the wonderful patchwork of cultural diversity at most campuses makes for some deeply rich offerings.

So, why not learn how to use chopsticks? Or use 'chopsticks' as a metaphor for learning a little something about ANY other culture? Take up

Bangra or Latin or Irish dancing (do you know why they don't move their upper body?). Attend a Passover Seder meal or a Cinco de Mayo celebration. Learn yoga or henna painting or origami. Try sushi or Thai or Indian or tapas food. Go see a gay pride parade or a step show or a hackathon.

The key here is to walk away from your first year with a greater understanding of someone else's culture or a new skill that complements and enhances your life – anything that makes you more interesting and fun and that helps you better understand at least one other person or group of people. For example, at dinner one night, a friend who grew up on an Iowa farm told of how he used to castrate pigs and make 'Rocky Mountain oysters.'* (Look 'em up!) You can even extend the idea to smaller sub-cultures and activities. Pick up a yo-yo, take up archery or rock-climbing or juggling, check out LARPing or anime or manga, but do something that allows you to walk away from your first year a more culturally aware, and culturally adept, person.**

The beauty of learning these things on a college campus is that you can just as easily learn them from a friend down the hall as from an organized activity or event. See your college community as a rich panoply of cultures just waiting to teach you about the world. Don't let it go untapped. *Carpe College!*

---

* Cultural confession: Although this made for fascinating dinner conversation, I have never been able to convince myself to try them. I have not been able to 'carpe' in this regard.

** I learned to juggle in the dorm hallway during my first year. A guy named Paul taught me. Thanks Paul! Paul also preferred juggling and smoking pot to studying. He did not return for year two. Know thyself, have a plan…yada, yada

DON'T HATE
THE MATE!

The roommate situation, it's just like,
I figured if me and Sam are together, we're gonna smush,
so let me not get myself into that situation.

— RONNIE, 'JERSEY SHORE'

Raise your hand if you shared a room with a sibling growing up. Yep, not too many of you!

The truth is that families got smaller over the last half century as the baby boom generation had fewer children. That meant that the baby boomers' kids (the 'Millennials' or 'Generation Y') did not have the luxury of sharing a bedroom growing up. Now those kids are heading off to college to live in rooms smaller than their own and dividing them in half to share with another kid who also never had to share. Not exactly a recipe for success! But that trend does not appear to be changing anytime soon.

Trends aside, it's vitally important to make every attempt to ensure that your roommate relationship is a positive one. Regardless of whether you're used to sharing a room or not, you're going to have to live with it... literally. To put a finer point on it, your dorm and your roommate will become your new home and family, the place and people you return to daily. If there's trouble at 'home,' it can infect every other aspect of your existence, and that can become a great burden as you attempt to tackle the new academic and social terrain of college life.

So, how can a couple of new college kids (or more if you end up in a triple or quad room) live peaceably together without too much turmoil? Moreover, how can you grow to really like and appreciate each other and cultivate a lasting friendship? Well, it's a bit of a crapshoot, and chance plays a big role in how these relationships go. You've got two people heading into a significant new stage of life in dramatically new surroundings with new intellectual and social demands, and then you give them 'their own space' but ask them to share it. Yeah, that's going to be a challenge. But this challenge is exactly where to begin.

First, let's acknowledge that this new situation will be tough for each roommate. Therefore, you should head into the relationship understanding that you'll need to be EXTRA tolerant of each other. After that, it's best to employ a 'hope for the best but plan for the worst' strategy. You hope you will both get along, be enriched by each others' interests and perspectives, share laughs and thrilling memorable moments, and become lifelong buddies. On the other hand, you plan for the proverbial 'roommate from hell.'

As with most other aspects of this book, our mantra comes in handy:

Know thyself. Have a plan. Assume no one else cares.

It might also help to recognize that the *Jersey Shore's* Ronnie was wise beyond his years when he said, "...let me not get myself into that situation."

(NOTE: This 'situation' is not to be confused with Ronnie's *Jersey Shore* mate, Mike Sorrentino, aka 'The Situation.')

(NOTE ON THAT PREVIOUS NOTE: If you don't know what this *Jersey Shore* 'reality show' phenomenon was, then, I guess...uh... Look it up!)

HERE ARE SOME TIPS FOR AVOIDING...WELL...SITUATIONS:

Communicate. Communicate. Communicate.

Before, during, and after meeting your roommate, communication is key. BEFORE arriving on campus, the housing people will have you and your roommate fill out some sort of questionnaire to try to tap into your preferences and tendencies. This is a good start, but some of those questions are pretty lame, and *sometimes* the prospective roommates lie about how late they stay up, etc. More important, sometimes the roommates don't yet know what their tendencies will be because they will be in new surroundings. So, I've developed a simpler questionnaire that gets right to the heart of *most* trouble spots. BEFORE meeting your roommate(s), share your honest answers to these questions (see *Appendix B* for a 'share sheet' you could use):

1. What smells bug you? (Body odor? Potpourri? Are you a fresh air freak where you'd rather have the window open in the winter time and wear a sweater than smell that thick, musty indoor air?)
2. What sounds bug you? (Screamo music? Only hearing one side of a phone conversation? Snoring? Alarm clock sounds? Toenail clipping?)

3. What sights bug you? (Messy spaces? Open curtains? Sunlight in the morning? Black-light posters? Cat posters? The color yellow? Old tennis shoes? Anything other than complete darkness when you sleep?)

4. What's your greatest fear or concern about your prospective room-mate(s)? (He's a Taylor Swift fan? She will bring boys into our room for 'extra-curricular activities?' He will play video games all day and never talk to me? She won't like it *when* I borrow her clothes?)

5. What are you like when at your worst? (When upset, do you shut down? Do you rage for five minutes and then want to be buds again? Are you a little passive aggressive? Does it help if someone brings you ice cream?)

NOTE: If you have trouble coming up with answers to these questions, you are going to be an incredibly tolerant roommate, and anyone would be glad to share space with you.

Answer the questions honestly and share your responses with your prospective roommate(s). If Taylor Swift or black-light posters or borrowing clothes will be a deal-breaker, it is absolutely best to figure that out sooner rather than later. In fact, having reflected on these things that bug you, maybe this is a good time to consider if they *really* are deal-breakers, or if, with a little bit of effort, they could fall within your expanded level of tolerance. If you think you could tolerate them, imagine doing so *every* day for the *entire* school year. That should be a good indicator. Again, know thyself.

Okay, let's say that you've gone through this 'deal-breaker vs. tolerance' exercise, and now you're settled in with your new roommate. As the first week kicks into gear, your focus naturally gets directed inward toward your own classes and trying to find your own bearings, so you and your room-mate don't pay that much attention to each other. Your schedules don't match, so you don't see as much of each other either. You do, however, begin to notice some of each others' little idiosyncrasies or habits. (Why does she leave her toothbrush out on her desk to dry out?! Why did he draw a mustache on the mirror, so he can imagine himself growing one each morning?!) Under normal circumstances, you might just talk to your room-mate about these little issues, but you have all this new stuff on your plate with your classes, and you don't want one more thing to have to deal with. So, you avoid it. Now, if each roommate is avoiding conversations, you may become like 'two ships that pass in the night,' where you don't talk much, you just occupy the same room.

This would be the beginnings of a bad development. So...

Break Bread

When you first meet, sit down with your roommate(s), look over your schedules, and pick one day each week when you can eat dinner together. This will be a great way to 'manufacture' an excuse to communicate and keep that relationship open and healthy. If the year goes smoothly and you get along famously, then your regular dinner date will simply be something you look forward to each week. If things don't go as smoothly, and the relationship gets rocky or distant, a weekly dinner will be the healthy prescription that allows you to be civil toward each other, to better understand each other, to air grievances and resolve them before they become bitter. Having dinner, breaking bread, has a way of humanizing people. Many believe that if enemies could dine together, it would alter their perspectives, effect compromise, and even bring about peace. Very few roommates ever become 'enemies' per se, but they sometimes become objects of frustration and contempt. Breaking bread can help prevent this possibility.

Truthfully Tackle the Tough Stuff

If your roommate has her boyfriend over and they're repeatedly engaging in behavior that makes you uncomfortable, you have to tell her. And there's only one way to do that: tell her. Wait for your weekly dinner and serve it up like this:

> *"Jenny, I've got something we need to hash out. Lately, you and John have been hanging out in the room a lot, and hanging all over each other. It makes me uncomfortable. I've found myself avoiding our room because of it, and I'd like to find some sort of solution. I realize this is news to you, so we don't have to solve it right now, but I just thought I should let you know how I feel."*

What you've done is told Jenny openly and honestly what her behavior is, how it's affecting you, and that you want it figured out. Moreover, you have given her time to think about it by saying that you don't have to resolve it right away, and that should relieve some pressure on her (she shouldn't feel completely besieged). But you have been clear, and now you can be open to her ideas for solutions. It's possible that she'll be ready to resolve it right then and there by apologizing and making a plan to alter the way she behaves. If so, be prepared to express what you feel will be an acceptable solution. If she's not willing to compromise significantly, you can at least try to forge some compromise including:

- Limiting the time she and her boyfriend spend in the room (maybe half their time could be spent in HIS room – and you could ask what

HIS roommate's thoughts are. Maybe he's already expressed displeasure from his end?)

• A notification system where you and Jenny let each other know WHEN you'll be in the room, so cuddling (spooning?) with John won't be part of the mix.

For most roommates in most situations, the aforementioned approach will resolve most issues. If a situation becomes dire, however, and she refuses to compromise at all, there are still more options...

Recruit Your RA (Resident Assistant)

Each floor or dorm area has a Resident Assistant, an older student who keeps a lid on things and tries to ensure that everyone lives respectfully and peaceably together. Sometimes they have to be the dorm 'cop' and deal with people who violate rules, but they are also trained in interpersonal communication to assist roommates if conflicts arise. If your roommate becomes too difficult, and all of your communication attempts have been thwarted, then recruit your RA to mediate your next conversation.

Contact your RA, tell her the history of your roommate challenges, and ask her to set up a meeting with all three of you present. Your RA will take the lead, and it will help to have an objective, third party in the mix. Of course, you'll communicate to your roommate that this was a last resort because your other attempts fell on deaf ears. Now you'll have another set of ears to hear it all.

NOTE: Of course, when human beings are involved, nothing is as simple as it sounds. It's possible that Jenny's boyfriend wasn't supposed to be in the dorm after midnight, and they were violating the dorm rules. So, you might hesitate to report this to your RA because then there could be more serious consequences for them, and that wasn't ever your intention... Yep! That's how dicey this can get. So, get creative. Tell the RA only the stuff that REALLY matters (the discomfort you feel) and avoid the stuff that might cause Jenny too much trouble (that she and her boyfriend were 'breaking the rules'). Then, after the three of you meet, maybe Jenny will recognize that you didn't throw her under the bus, and she will adjust her behavior to accommodate you.

If Jenny still doesn't adjust, your RA can advise you on next steps.

You Are Not Henry Higgins

Remember him? He's the guy who tried to train Eliza Doolittle to say, "The rain in Spain stays mainly in the plain" properly. (Look it up.) He got her 'trained' and then fell in love with her, but there was much wailing and gnashing of teeth along the way. It's important to note that it's not your job to fix your roommate, and if you did, you still may not fall in love with the results. Every roommate has little neuroses or idiosyncrasies and, if they're not over the top, don't worry over them. If your roommate is consistently messy or late, you might just have to let him be messy or late. If she talks too much, try listening. Consider accepting your roommate 'warts and all.' You might be pleasantly surprised what you learn about them and what you learn about yourself in the process. Or, as Henry Higgins put it, you might "grow accustomed to her face."

Summon the Safety Net

If you and your roommate are open and honest, you've tried every healthy way to resolve conflicts and differences (even asking your RA to mediate), and you still can't come to tolerate each other, then it's time to move on. Your residence hall service is equipped to handle these situations, and your RA will be able to help you facilitate a move.

The absolute worst case would be if there were NO other opens slots in any other dorms on campus. Typically, however, your RA can find at least one other set of roommates who would be looking to switch.

The key is that you have exhausted all other avenues to try to rectify the situation. The housing folks make this a point of emphasis, mostly because it's a hassle and logistical nightmare to move people around, so they don't like to do it, but also because they want you to develop the requisite skills to navigate through such difficult interpersonal waters (at least that's what they'll tell you).

FINISHING STRONG

Whew!! Slogging through all of that was heavy. And it will be if you end up having roommate troubles. So, let's end with a positive scenario, one in which you've hoped for the best and got it....

You arrive at your dorm room as the school year is about to begin, and your new roommate Mark has already moved in, given you the bed by the window (just as you had talked about on Facebook), where he left you a little welcome gift of Cracker Jack and a Gatorade from the campus store. Next to that, there's a little hand-written note saying, *"Hey, Tom, I got here early, but I didn't start moving around any of the furniture 'cause I figured we should do that together. See you soon, Roomie! (Sorry, about the 'Roomie' thing. I'm not really that lame. I just always wanted to say that. Now I'll stop!)"*

You eventually meet Mark, you guys hit it off by sharing Art History notes, playing intramural soccer, and partying together. He's from California, so he invites you home for spring break, and you make the same offer and bring him to New York the following year. You end up getting an apartment together after sophomore year, getting season football tickets together, and doing summer abroad in Australia. Later on, you'll stand up in each other's weddings, but we don't need to lay it on that thick yet.

The point is that, for most roommates, things can be pretty darn smooth and, sometimes, downright rich and delightful!

Again, hope for the best and plan for the worst. Anything in between – which is most likely – will be completely manageable.

SPEAKING OF RICH, HOW ABOUT SOME ROOMMATE ROYALTY?

One interesting upside to sharing living space with someone else is the potential for some magical mojo to creep into roommate relationships and pay dividends later. Rich, lifelong relationships can develop. You can push each other, help each other, and enrich each other. An off-the-cuff comment during a roommate chat may be the inspirational spark that compels one to change majors, get more serious about school, or become rededicated to an outside passion. Or you could both have the right stuff to become famous. Who knows? You and your roommate could be the next Tommy Lee Jones and Al Gore.

Here's a list of famous roommate pairs:
Actor Tommy Lee Jones & Vice President Al Gore (Harvard)
Actors Robin Williams & Christopher Reeve (Julliard)
Film collaborators Owen Wilson & Wes Anderson (Texas)
ESPN analyst Lee Corso & actor Burt Reynolds (Florida State)
Actors Holly Hunter & Frances McDormand (Yale)
Actors Parker Posey & Sherry Stringfield (SUNY Purchase)
Super Bowl Champion Coach Tony Dungy & NBA Coach Flip Saunders
    (Minnesota)
Senator Lamar Alexander & NFL Commissioner Paul Tagliabue (NYU Law)
New York Governor Eliot Spitzer & TV host Jim Cramer (Harvard Law)
NCAA Champion Coach Jim Boeheim & Super Bowl Champion Coach
    Tom Coughlin (Sort of… Boeheim was Coughlin's RA at Syracuse)

ONE FINAL NOTE ABOUT TREATING SPECIAL ROOMMATE CASES SPECIALLY.

What if you decide to room with a 'friend from home?' Well, there are good and bad ways this could go. The good: You already know each other well, you've even traveled together and spent time in close quarters, you share similar interests, and you get along. This means you won't have all those 'getting to know you issues' others will have. The bad: You might begin to grate on each others' nerves now that you live together, that could degrade your friendship, and you could fall into the all-too-common trap of sticking too closely to your social comfort zone and not branching out to meet new people. Imagine if the two of you stuck closely together, didn't meet new people, and THEN got tired of each other. To whom would you turn?

Recommendation: Choose to room with someone new. Have that rich and challenging experience. And stay in touch with your friend from home. You both will have your new roommates AND new circles of dorm friends, and then you can introduce everyone to each other, thereby doubling the new people you meet. Wow! Not a bad plan.

If you chose to room with a friend from home, BE SURE to force yourselves to branch out and meet new people. You're already playing it safe with your roommate choice. Don't do the same with the rest of your social experience once you arrive on campus.

QUICK TIPS FOR ROOMMATE SURVIVAL

"Fish and visitors smell after three days."

— BEN FRANKLIN

So, all of that preceding chapter was about planning for the worst and hoping for the best. Here's a 'quick tips' approach to living well with your roomie for more than three days....

AVOID ALARM ANNOYANCES

The surest way to create roommate tension is a lack of alarm clock management. If you tend to sleep through your alarm or incessantly slap the snooze button, you may be in for some trouble with your roommate. If you 'wake the bear,' and if you keep doing so, eventually the bear will turn on you.

One solution might be to use your cell phone alarm and plug earphones into it, so when you awake, it doesn't wake anyone else. Another solution is to simply shut off your alarm the *first* time it rings. While both of these are *reasonable* solutions for most *reasonable* people, they may not be successful for you if you're the kind of person who falls back asleep right after turning off your alarm. For that, you'll need another strategy.

The best way to avoid falling back to asleep is to get to your feet as soon as possible. The best way to get to your feet as soon as possible is to place your alarm far away from your bed. This way, you'll feel compelled to shut it off, so it doesn't bother your roommate (who will kick you out – or kick your ass – if you don't). You'll jump out of bed, and by the time the alarm is off, you're on your feet and ready to head off to the shower. If, on the other hand, you simply jump back into bed, then you might as well stay there and enjoy the ride. You'll probably flunk out, but you'll get plenty of beauty rest in the process.

T-SHIRT TRIVIA

Alarms buzzing, slivers of sunlight at 6am, a roommate's tardy typing at 2am, or a snoring suitemate can all become the most annoying and grating sounds in the world if you're trying to sleep. Of course, they typically inject themselves when you least expect them and most need your sleep. There is, however, a cheap and effective fix: the t-shirt. That's right! All college kids have 'em, but not all know how to use 'em. They can become your best friend, a 'sensory silencer,' when you most need it. Here's how:

Lay any t-shirt out flat on your bed. Fold in the arms across the torso, so that the cloth becomes a rectangle. Beginning at either the left or right side of the shirt, roll it into a loose 'log'. You now have God's greatest gift to humankind... if you're trying to sleep, that is. Lie down with your head on your pillow, take your new 'sensory silencer' and lay it across both eyes with the extra cloth hanging down the sides of your face. Take these sides and cover your ears, tucking any excess in behind your ears between your head and pillow. That's it. You'll notice all the sensory deprivation (or at least the muffling of all sights and sounds) right away! Try it this summer before you head off to campus. If you aren't satisfied with the results, you may not return this book, and you will not receive a full refund. You can figure out your own damn strategy.

(Hey! Maybe I should have some *"Carpe College!"* t-shirts made up, and you could use those. Then, if not satisfied, you'd have another nice, colorful, non-refundable item you could not return, not ever.)

NOTE: I recently confirmed this t-shirt thing really works! I was in a hotel in LA, sleeping with my 'sensory silencer' over my eyes and ears. At 3am flashing strobe lights on every alarm in the hotel suite went off, but the alarms remained silent. I did not wake up until I heard my wife on the phone with the front desk, trying to figure out what the heck was going on. So, yes, I did hear my wife through the muffling of the shirt, but I did not see all those strobe lights. Apparently, my 'silencer' method blocks light better than sound, but I contend that it's way more comfortable than any eye mask or ear plugs. Try it for yourself.

STOCK-UP ON SUPPLIES

Ear plugs, eye masks, earphones (and extras because they tend to wear out), your mp3 player, the aforementioned 'sensory silencer' t-shirt roll, and an extra pillow are all great supplies to have when it comes to avoiding things that go bump in the night (or morning). If your roomie is an early riser, needs a bit of light to get dressed or, God forbid, blow dries her hair at 6am, then you may need some sensory protection. Have this stuff at the ready for those manic mornings (or late nights) when you want to sleep but your roommate doesn't.

Of course, the BEST strategies and solutions involve communicating with your roommate and getting healthy, consistent sleep and exercise so you can wake refreshed (with no alarm 'snoozing'). If both of you are doing that, all will be right with the world.

NO SWEAT?

College kids these days are working out and staying more physically fit than ever before. It may be because they want to look healthy or simply be healthy, or because many campuses have nice fitness facilities. Whatever the reason, it's probably a good thing. But those sweaty clothes need to go somewhere.

In our household, with both our kids in high school athletics and working out on their own, our laundry room got pretty darn stinky. It got to the point where we put a hamper in the garage and threw all the sweaty stuff in there until we could do a load of wash during our busy week. When our son went off to college, his fitness lifestyle didn't change; however, his dorm room living quarters were about as small as our laundry room, so those wonderful aromas had much less space in which to waft away.

As we discussed how to handle sweaty clothes in dorm rooms, my wife and I couldn't remember how we did it in college, other than to simply throw them in our closets. We did remember, however, that our rooms did NOT smell, which, my wife assures me, is NOT the case with my son's dorm room (as of this writing, I have not yet been allowed in my son's dorm room. My wife talked her way in when picking him up for winter break because he needed an extra set of hands to carry dirty laundry). So, we tossed out some ideas for managing this olfactory obstacle, and here are my thoughts:

113

1. Have three (3) laundry bags: one that's mesh for the 'sweaty-smellies' to air out, one that's nylon and doesn't breathe (or a plastic garbage bag will do), and one that's cloth or anything else to carry your stuff down to the laundry facility. When empty, put the first two bags inside the third and keep it under your bed or in your closet.

2. After working out, when you come home dripping with sweat, remove your 'sweaty-smellies' and turn them all right-side out (do not leave socks or anything else rolled up in a ball). Clip it all to a hanger, a makeshift clothesline, or your mesh bag AND HANG THAT WET STUFF OUTSIDE YOUR DORM WINDOW TO AIR OUT! Now, depending on your windows, your residence hall policies, or the weather, you may have to get creative. If you're on the fourth floor, maybe you can tie the drawstring onto your desk leg with a bungee cord or something. If dorm policies prevent hanging stuff out your window (a STRONG possibility), maybe you can hang your clothes in your open window with a fan on them until they're dried out. If it's raining, or you're worried about your wet clothes freezing and then melting and reeking once back safe and sound in your room, then, obviously, you'll need to dry them indoors over a chair or your bed rail.

   The key is, whatever you do, you must get them dry! Although I'm an old-school cotton kind of guy, you may wish to start with synthetic sweat-wicking clothing, which will dry much quicker.

3. Once your 'sweaty-smellies' are dry and aired out, throw them into a nylon bag (or plastic garbage bag) that doesn't breathe. Scrunch down the bag, so there's very little air in it, and seal it tight. That way, all that nastiness can't waft throughout your small dorm room. (If the clothes only reek a little after drying, then toss 'em into that mesh bag with a fabric softener sheet to mask the odor a bit.) If you continue to work out and have new 'sweaty-smellies,' just repeat the process, again and again, until laundry day.

   NOTE: My sister-in-law contends that if there's even a little bit of moisture, the clothes will mildew, smell, and continue to smell every time they get wet again. She may be right, but she's also a little overly sensitive. She thinks it's a bad idea to eat stuff out of the fridge without checking expiration dates, too. But we all know that the smell test works better. If food smells, don't eat it. If clothes smell, don't wear 'em. Or, better yet, just clean 'em.

4. On laundry day, throw the nylon bag of 'sweaty-smellies' into your main laundry bag, and head down to the machines. Separate your clothes as you see fit, and enjoy the results. It's as simple as that!

Of course, I'm still waiting for some innovative and entrepreneurial spirit to develop a better system. Maybe your campus fitness facility could implement a system where you toss your 'sweaty-smellies' into a mesh wash bag with a number on it, bring that bag to the locker room check out desk, they do the wash for you, and you pick up your workout clothes the next time you stop in. The same way you check out a basketball or badminton racquet, you'd check in and out your workout clothes.

Maybe not... We're just spitballin' here...

CLEANLINESS IS NEXT TO GODLINESS?

Invite people into your dorm room at least once a month. That way, you and your roommate(s) will clean your room at least that often. If you have no idea how to do this, ask your folks, ask your roommate's folks, or walk up and down the dorm hall until you find someone who can help. Or, maybe there's a YouTube tutorial or app for that! Hadn't even thought about that until just now because this is stuff you should already know. (Look it up!)

If you need more motivational help, visit unfuckyourhabitat.com, a website acknowledging that we all have busy lives, or are just lazy, and need a little push. So they offer "terrifying motivation for lazy people with messy homes." Oh, and they even have an app for that.

Any way you choose, figure it out and clean your damn room!

DON'T TOUCH IT OR BORROW IT WITHOUT ASKING!

Not her snacks. Not his laptop. Not her favorite top. Not his Frisbee. No, no, no... Again, this is stuff you should already know.

STAY GOLD, PONYBOY

To survive and thrive in a college dorm room, just follow The Golden Rule: Do unto others as you would have them do unto you (or anything close to that). 'Nuff said...

Or, if that's not enough said, then take a peek at P.M. Forni's *Choosing Civility: The Twenty-Five Rules of Considerate Conduct*. It has everything from "Listen" to "Don't shift responsibility and blame," and plenty in between.

★★★

SPECIAL NOTE: David Foster Wallace was a great author who died too young. Before he left us, he gave a commencement speech that gets at the heart of what it means to live with other people and how we can CHOOSE to hate it or celebrate it (Hey, that rhymes... I should be a rapper!) Wallace called his speech "This is Water," and a few people have made short films to accompany it. (Look it up!)

FIVE-ALARM
MAC-N-CHEESE

(aka Just Add Water & Don't Be the Perp)

Okay.... So.... Aside from complaints about laundry room etiquette, there's nothing that gets college dorm dwellers more pissed off than being awakened by a fire alarm at 3am. The only thing that makes it worse is when everyone hears the reason was a fire in the microwave because someone didn't add water to his mac 'n cheese or tend to her popcorn.

"Are you f★★★ing kidding me?!"* can be heard careening through the quad when the word gets out. "Who's the a★★hole who never learned how to use a microwave?!"* And the perpetrator had better lie low for the next few days because no one will be happy. Some people will have exams in the morning. Some will have just gotten to bed. Some might be 'sleeping where they shouldn't be.' No one will be thrilled about clearing the halls and standing outside until the fire marshal finds the source of the trouble.

Do yourself a favor and don't be the perp!

Add water. Read labels. Learn some basic cooking skills before you get to college. And, for goodness sake, friends don't let friends cook drunk! This is usually how mac-n-cheese gets burned in a microwave.

If, for some reason, you do something stupid like this, go back and re-read the section about Forgive, Fix It, and Forge Ahead. That should get you through.

(Oh... One more thing. Since this chapter focused on cooking, don't 'Fake Bake' either. That artificial tanning stuff is really bad for you. Look it up!)

---

* Mark Twain said, "The difference between the right word and the nearly right word is the difference between lightning and the lightning bug." The colorful language used above is most definitely the right words for this occasion. Mos Def!

PARTY LIKE A SMARTY

(aka Don't Make the News!)

*"I have been drunk for almost a week now,
so I thought it might sober me up to sit in a library."*

— F. SCOTT FITZGERALD

"In vino veritas" was a phrase I learned in Latin class (yes, I went to school in the middle ages), meaning "In wine there is truth." One possible interpretation is that drinking will bring out your true colors. It'll 'help' you say things you might otherwise keep to yourself, or try things you might otherwise not try. This could be good or this could be bad. You'll have to figure out your own 'truth' on this count. You have been around the block enough, however, to know that people drink, and drinking complicates matters. But let's start with something more positive.

How 'bout a list of things alcohol makes easier....

Talking to strangers ✓
Talking to attractive people typically out of your league ✓
Getting laid by these people (uh, nope!)
Getting laid by people who consider you out of their league ✓
Getting mugged ✓
Falling asleep ✓
Waking up (uh, nope!)
Having the next drink and the next ✓
Wetting yourself ✓
Having sex ✓
Having good sex (uh, nope!)
Trying new food combinations ✓
Texting tactfully (uh, nope!)
Throwing up that 3AM burrito you shouldn't have had in the first place ✓
Keeping the weight off (uh, nope!)
Thinking straight (uh, nope!)
Thinking you're thinking straight ✓
Getting an ambulance ride to the hospital ✓

Okay, so maybe that didn't turn out to be entirely positive. With alcohol in the mix, keeping it entirely positive can be tough and it requires more thought.

Remember our mantra? *Know thyself. Have a plan. Assume no one else cares.* Well, this mantra doesn't always work in the context of the partying scene because people start drinking and don't really "know themselves." Also, their best-laid plans fly out the window. Your 'buddy system' breaks down when people start hooking up and splintering off. The only part of the mantra that sticks is "no one cares."

Let's be real. We all know how it works. You gather up your dorm mates, about six or eight guys and girls, and you light out for that Friday night house party you heard about. You all say the right things on the way there, like "Kayla, you are NOT leaving my side tonight!" and "Bobby, I'm your wingman!" But you get to the party, have a few drinks, and before you know it, everybody's hooking up or going to another party, and you lose track of each other. This is the beginning of the end. The best-laid party plans break down, and the consequences can be devastating. People don't just get lost in an entertaining "Dude, where did you go last night?" kind of way. People can get hurt, seriously hurt. Those worst-case scenarios of alcohol poisoning, drowning, and sexual assault aren't just fiction; they are based on some reality.

However, we don't have to be paralyzed by fears, and these breakdowns don't need to be some dire commentary on your friendships and loyalty. It's just the nature of the beast when it comes to the college social scene, and smart behavior will alleviate most concerns.

HERE IS MY PERSONAL REQUEST LIST TO HELP YOU PARTY LIKE A SMARTY:

PLEASE know your limits (and stick to them)

It's okay to say, "Three beers and I'm done!" or "No shots tonight!" or, I don't know, "I'll just have water." I have a friend who found out that he could not handle tequila. He realized (after only a couple of encounters) that, when he drank tequila, he would end up sleepwalking and be oblivious to it in the morning. Once, he was awakened by the sound of his apartment complex door slamming behind him. He had sleepwalked outside onto the lawn in his underwear only to have the door lock behind him. Needless to say, he did NOT have a key handy under these circumstances. He learned his limits and stopped drinking tequila. Know thyself.

PLEASE have a 'SOBER SOLDIER'

Before you head out, and with a stern loyalty pact, assign one of your group to remain sober and lucid for the evening. This person's job is to ensure that everyone remains safe for the entire evening till they're nestled snuggly in their beds. Obviously, this duty should be on a rotating system with everyone taking turns. An enhanced plan would also include a 'buddy system' where you're all partnered up in addition to the watchful eye of your 'sober soldier.' If this sounds too lame, try following the lead of those guys in *The Hangover* movies and see how that works for you.

No one has solved the binge-drinking problem yet. It's not just about drinking to get drunk. It's about games and fun, and it's highly social. It's also highly dangerous, and there is a definite 'mob mentality' to it, where no one in the mob is thinking clearly about the behaviors of the mob. So, in these circumstances, more than ever, someone needs to be looking out for you.

You know the drill: Friends don't let friends… etc. For everyone's sake, please abide by it.

PLEASE make it 'Your Pour'

If you go to a party and decide to drink something, make sure that you open it and you pour it! It's horrendous, but there are too many cases these days of people lacing drinks with drugs designed to make drinkers lose control of their faculties. If it's beer from a keg, you pour it. If it's a can or a bottle, you open it. To be safe, you need to be in control of what you're drinking. Community punch bowls or red Solo cups lined up already full of beer can be a recipe for real trouble.

Here's a true and complicated story to illustrate the point....

One of my male students asked me to be an advocate for him at a disciplinary hearing because of a party misstep. He went to a party with friends and they met a small group of female students. They chatted briefly, and he offered to grab drinks for the group. He went downstairs and took cups of beer that had already been poured from a keg and lined up on a counter. He delivered the beers to the group, eventually got bored, and went home with a buddy. Apparently, by the end of the evening, one of the women got either very drunk or was drugged by something that was in her beer. She claimed the latter, and she accused my student of committing the act because he was the only person she could remember.

Obviously, it was a very ugly and scary experience for both of them. While it wasn't entirely preventable, these students could have made sure that they knew where their drinks came from.

PLEASE go blue

Walk home 'blue-light-to-blue-light,' utilizing those ubiquitous safety systems that exist on most campuses. They're light poles with glowing blue lights and a call box designed to give anyone quick access to emergency personnel. Now, evidence suggests that those blue light safety boxes may not be used as often as campus safety professionals would like, and there's lots of debate about their effectiveness in the age of cell phones. However, if your campus has 'em, why not use 'em?

(NOTE: One of my former students, Eric Irish, has actually developed a cell phone app that would create an "anywhere blue light" that users could push and connect directly to their campus safety system. It's called CampusSafe. Look it up.)

PLEASE don't go it alone

After nightfall, you should never walk alone, especially if you've been drinking. Let's just point out the obvious, that consuming alcohol affects your judgment and faculties. So, if there is danger, it stands to reason that you will be more compromised and vulnerable (and you'll be without friends).

It doesn't matter if you're the toughest guy on campus, if you've drunk too much and start staggering home, you can get hurt. Without even encountering anyone along the way, you could take a wrong turn and fall down by the river. Hit your head, and that could be all she wrote. It happens more often than you might think!

Now, let's assume you encounter four other drunk guys who had absolutely no notion of causing any trouble when they left. But now here you come, sloshing along and one of 'em can't resist tripping you. You attempt to 'fight' back. Things get rough. They pummel you and, just because the idea occurs to them spur of the moment, they take your wallet. If you're lucky, you'll find your way home and put some ice on your pain. If you're a bit unlucky, they've broken your jaw (or worse), and you'll be finding it hard to eat, let alone study, for the next month.

Shall we run through a scenario in which it's a drunk girl staggering home who encounters the four guys? I'd rather not.

I realize this can come across as 'blaming the victims.' I'd prefer to think of it as trying to prevent you from becoming a victim, although I realize there's no true prevention if bad people want to do bad things. The only one who can truly prevent a crime is the one committing it. However, we all can work toward limiting opportunities for bad stuff to happen. Of course, if someone assaults you, it's not your fault. They're the asshole! They committed the crime! But ever since you left the nest for your first time and your mother let you venture off to the playground on your own, you were taught to take precautions. This is simply an extension of these precautions in a new setting under new conditions. Think on it...

PLEASE go by the numbers

It's wise to pre-program all campus safety numbers into your phone. Do it during orientation, so you can be sure you're set from the beginning. In fact, I'd start with your orientation adviser and RA (they're good resources, of course, but they're also good for safety). Add your campus safety emergency, non-emergency, and health center numbers, and that should cover you in terms of 'official' people you might need to contact. (Also be sure you sign up for your campus safety alert system, so you get a cell phone alert when there is any safety concern on campus.)

As you make friends, you can also establish your own escort pact with them and have that group pre-programmed into your phone to call at a moment's notice. However, if someone says their number is 867-5309, you shouldn't trust 'em. (If you didn't get that last bit, try singing the number or google 'Bad 80's Songs'.)

If you follow these straightforward 'requests,' you'll avoid the greatest party dangers.

Here's one more thing to consider.... Remember those nice parents who helped you get to college and are maybe even footing the bill? The only time they want to see your name in the paper is when you make the dean's list, NOT on the heels of a wild weekend! In Arthur Miller's *The Crucible*, John Proctor refuses to sully his name by signing a statement that is a lie. He shouts, "Because it is my name. Because I cannot have another in my life... Leave me my name!"

Make sure that if your name is going to be in the paper, the news will be good. For you and for your folks!

★★★

NOTE: Did you know that underage drinking is illegal? True. Did you know that many college Presidents want to lower the drinking age to promote more-responsible drinking habits on campuses? (Look it up.)

THE LONGEST TITLE FOR THE SHORTEST CHAPTER ABOUT WALKING HOME ALONE AT NIGHT ON A COLLEGE CAMPUS

DON'T!

WADDYA MEAN, DON'T?!

It's simple. Drunk or sober, DON'T walk home alone at night (as mentioned briefly earlier). College campuses are pretty self-contained and safe places, for the most part, but that's why the few people 'flying solo' out at night become prime targets. If anyone wants to do harm, they're going after the lone wolf (or lamb). Please don't be lulled into a false sense of security. Anywhere you go, there is risk, and college campuses are no different. Crimes are the result of motive and opportunity, but you can take measures to limit those opportunities.

Assaults or thefts at the ATM machine, the bus stop, or even walking home from the library are not unheard of. Aside from the scary violence and violation of it all, they will affect the victim in a deep and prolonged way. Most of these incidents, however, can be mitigated by walking with friends or by taking advantage of the safety support most campuses provide, like escort or ride services.

Reach out to your friends or reach out to these services, but please reach out.

Carpe College

YOUR SEX OPTIONS

(aka Your Parents' Favorite Chapter)

KEEPING IT SIMPLE?

Here are your sex options:

1. Don't have sex
2. Practice safe sex

Do you really think it's that simple?! Of course not. Sex is as complex as the people who engage in it. At college campuses, it is, arguably, more complicated than other places. Begin with varying values about sex itself, sprinkle in youth, friendships, emerging self-discovery and gender relations, add a dash of drugs and alcohol and cramped living conditions, and we have a recipe for confusion, conflict and, potentially, pain.

At one end of the spectrum, we have the 'painless hook-up' where no one (allegedly) gets hurt. But at the other end of the spectrum, we have an alcohol-induced sexual assault that will mar the college experience and scar for life.

Given that you're vaulting yourself into your first serious and predominantly independent foray into running your own life, including college and career and all your future aspirations, you probably don't want sex to muck it up. Moreover, as an emerging adult, you probably want to begin to live your life in a respectable and respectful way. Have you given any serious thought to what 'respectable and respectful' might look like to you? What it might look like to others?

This sex stuff (and its aftermath) really can get in the way of your academics, you know. Whatever kind of reflection you have already given to your sex life, it is probably not enough. It should continue as you venture into your college years and, thankfully, campuses are well equipped to help you think about it. When you get to campus, you will be able to visit your campus health clinic or take part in campus-based programs promoting awareness and healthy behaviors. You should check 'em out.

If you don't think you need these resources, or you still have doubts about whether this sex stuff needs to be taken seriously, I'll close with a question that can be personal, philosophical and legal all at once:

What does consent look like?

Oh, wait. I've got a better one:

What does consent look like when one or both people have been drinking?

If you've got an easy answer for this, then you're good to go. Have your fun. If not, please continue to explore and reflect upon these issues.

Once again, our mantra applies:

Know Thyself. Have a Plan. Assume No One Else Cares.

I WANT YOUR SEX

For the sex researcher in you, try this. The world famous Kinsey Institute for Research on Sex, Gender and Reproduction offers you a chance to record and report your own and others' sex related activities through their Kinsey Reporter App. So, if you're engaged in anything from kissing to cuddling to copulating, or you see others engaged in similar acts, you can report it on the spot. The app captures data on these myriad behaviors to show what's going on in your town, your state, or around the globe. Check it out at kinseyreporter.org.

Ah, technology!

SPEAKING OF SEX BEHAVIORS, WHAT ABOUT WHEN IT'S NO LONGER SEX?

We have not really addressed sexual assault here, but it is gravely serious, and it is a hot topic on campuses today. (Look it up!) Sexual assaults do happen on college campuses, and more occur than are reported. Most are committed by someone known to the victim, and they involve alcohol. So, my previous 'don't walk home alone' admonishment isn't really adequate here.

In fact, nothing I can do with a sub-section of this book will be adequate, so you'll need to turn elsewhere to educate yourself and put yourself in the best possible position to deal with this very complex and serious issue.

For a just-scratching-the-surface cursory look at this very complex issue, here are some articles that emerged during the writing of this book:

In July 2013, a Kate Taylor article in the *New York Times* entitled "Sex on Campus: She Can Play That Game Too" took a stab at delving into the sex-at-school terrain. It opened up a real can o' worms, there was much chatter, and Lauren Ingeno followed up with a piece in *Inside Higher Ed* called "Let's talk (differently) About Sex," which tried to add some more color. Both are interesting reading. (Look 'em up!)

In October 2013, Emily Yoffe wrote a piece for *Slate* entitled, "College Women: Stop Getting Drunk," suggesting that we are reluctant to tell women to cease with this behavior that is so closely tied to sexual assault. Her colleague, Amanda Hess responded with a piece arguing that the focus should be on the rapists, not the victims. And Yoffe responded in turn about the connections to binge-drinking and her view that it is part of the normal maturation process to learn to restrain pleasure-seeking behaviors in order to avoid dangers. (Look 'em up!)

Serious people are thinking seriously about this stuff. You should too.

CLAMORING
FOR
COMMUNITY

For a book that's supposed to be positive and embrace all the wonderful offerings of college life, we have spent the last several pages talking about some truly difficult matters. From drinking to other dangers, there is no prevention panacea. A college campus is, first and foremost, a community, and it can fall prey to the same problems that plague any community. There is a perception, however, that college campuses should be safer, that they should, in some way, rise to higher ground aspiring to be 'better than that.'

Well, they are generally safe, and they do aspire to be better. They prefer to mold conscientious and thoughtful citizens. They prefer to converse openly and honestly in order to resolve conflict. And they prefer to create a campus culture so enlightened that transgressions such as assaults are prevented. In most cases, they do a pretty good job of it. For many campuses, they do a far better job than other communities. However, college campuses still have a police presence for a reason. They still serve and protect and arrest and have students removed from the community for violating rules. They are communities made up of human beings and, no matter how hard they might aspire to loftier living, any individual on any given day may not buy into those aspirations and may cause harm.

You simply cannot put that many newly-independent young people in close living quarters with intense social dynamics (and beer!), and expect it to all be pretty. You can, however, as my former student Jill suggests, expect a campus community to DECIDE that they want to be kind and look out for each other. You can DECIDE to report the belligerent drunk guy or that stranger lurking around your building. You can DECIDE to stop and help the student stumbling home alone. You can DECIDE to limit opportunities for harm and intervene when harm is happening.

So, just like these campuses that hold lofty ideals but recognize the need for some practical protections, you too can hope for the best but plan for the worst. You can also educate yourself by learning more about reported crimes on college campuses through the Clery Center for Security on Campus, and you can become more informed about sexual violence through the National Sexual Violence Resource Center (Look them up!)

I'm reminded of how my father, a Chicago cop for thirteen years who had seen his share of trouble, used to advise his children. "If you see trouble, walk the other way!" he would say. Now, that was a parent looking out for the welfare of his kids. Although I respect my dad's motives, I think I like Jill's approach a bit more. It will require courage, but when trouble occurs, stepping up and helping, or using your phone to call for assistance before using it to record the incident, should make for a better and safer campus environment.

It should make for a community.

LAUNDRY LESSONS:

"I never let laundry get in the way of my education."

— MARK TWAIN (-ISH)

We're not going to spend time suggesting spin-cycle strategies or breaking down brights vs. colors here. If you've got complicated clothes-cleaning criteria, then you should already have a well-established laundry attack plan, and you don't need this chapter. (Besides, the next few pages evolve into more than just laundry.)

For the rest of you, here's the simplest washing machine formula:

Whites in Warm. *
Everything else in cold. **

That's it. Two loads. Get in and get out. If you're gonna *Carpe College!*, you can't spend too much time and energy on laundry. (Can you tell this was written by a guy?!) Plus, there are much more important laundry room lessons to learn that have nothing to do with getting clothes clean, and we will focus on those here. For whatever reason (e.g. smaller families, helicopter parents serving the every need of their millennial children, fear of confined quarters), many incoming college students encounter some hard facts of life when doing laundry, particularly in a dorm setting. We will call them 'The Laundry Lessons,' and here's episode one....

In your typical household, if you want some laundry done, the 2.6 children holler loudly, and a mother-type person retrieves articles of clothing to commence with load upon load until everyone's reasonably happy. Not so in the dormitory!

---

* Tree-hugging environmentalists do things differently (i.e. everything in cold). College is a great time to experiment on this front, too.

** Apparently, the experts say that most detergents are only activated in temperatures 65-degrees F and warmer, but most cold cycles are between 65- and 80-degrees F. So, you should be covered.

Your first venture down to the basement bowels of Boozer Hall may find a packed house with NO washers available, and every dryer warmin' and spinnin'. You thought for sure you could venture down on a Sunday night and wash what you needed to start your week. But, alas, so did a dozen other people (because you're all bright, after all…and used to getting your way).

So, you go to Plan B: Doing your wash at 6am Monday when no one else is thinking about it. Good idea, but your alarm goes off, and you dose off… And Plan B is now off.

Plan C: How 'bout biting the bullet for another five days and, when everyone's partying on Friday at midnight, you'll head down and load your laundry in. Ooops… Someone else had the same strategy and, WHOA, is she pretty! She's got one of those braids that hangs down across one shoulder, and oh, she's reading a book… and she appears to be reading for fun! So, she's got the depth factor. Man, she's out of your league on so many counts! But back to the laundry… She's cleared the washers and moved all her belle-of–the-ball belongings into ALL six of the dryers. She's a woMAN with a PLAN, and it apparently involves much segregation and sorting during the drying phase of the laundry process. While you're thinking about how to strike up a conversation, you're also thinking about how much you're starting to hate this laundry stuff. And the whole 'pretty girl with quirky laundry habits' is creating unnecessary consternation.

Then, before you have time to put two thoughts together, she bolts from the laundry room, leaving just you, your wash, and her tumbling tube tops behind. (Are those retro enough to be back in fashion?!) Well, after you crack open your calculus for the next half hour, we can flash forward to the part where her dryers have run their course. They're done, but she hasn't returned. And then, of course, moments later, your wash loads are done and ready to be dried. And, as we said, she has NOT returned to clear her dryers.

So, now, my friend, you are faced with what we like to call a dilemma. Do you:

- A). Wait and waste away the rest of your Friday (now Saturday)?
- B). Wander to look for her and waste away the rest of your Friday (now Saturday)?
- C). Remove her clothes quickly and toss them on the counter, touching them as little as possible?
- D). Remove her clothes and fold them carefully, realizing that you will be touching them a lot… including those…um… how do you say?… more private items?

E). Remove and fold them carefully, but take some time to smell them to ensure freshness?

OKAY, if you're even considering E, then you're too dumb to be in college. Give this book back to whoever gave it to you, so they can re-gift it!

If you chose A through D, they're all fine, but you're on your own. I don't have any answers to this dilemma. You could be damned if you do and damned if you don't on all counts. You could also make a brand new friend, or meet your wife for life. I have no idea. I am not an expert, after all. There's no such thing as expertise when it comes to *Carpe College!* You just carpe!

What I do know is that this kind of living arrangement with its peculiar people and sharing of space and personal plans and consistent collisions of daily affairs is a supreme challenge. You're going to have to navigate it with respect for others and respect for yourself. You can't be a jerk or a doormat. You'll need a happy medium.

Okay, if you absolutely must have a firm answer, flip a coin and select either C or D. If she returns and you have some explainin' to do, just be genuine. You were just trying to help. Anything this side of a slap in the face is a win in our book.

Look... This is DIFFICULT stuff, people! That's right. Like most of college, it's all about people. All flawed and fallible and trying to find their way. You're gonna have to learn to deal with 'em all and live peaceably.

That's why there are so many tough lessons to learn surrounding laundry. Toss that in your spin-cycle and smoke it!

TEENAGE WASTELAND

"They're All Wasted!"

— PETE TOWNSHEND, THE WHO'S *BABA O'RILEY*

"Time passes. Will you?" At some point in your middle or high school years, you probably encountered this little ditty posted near the classroom clock by some extra-clever and 'punny' teacher. It actually is quite clever to remind any clock-watching students that they are wasting time by checking the clock.

At college, however, there are no quaint and clever reminders. There's just you. So, you need to identify the time-wasters, know them by name, and master them so that they do not master you. Here are the big ones:

- Surfing the web
- Texting
- Socializing
- Facebook & other social media
- Movies & TV (or, better yet, can you say YouTube?!)
- Video games (you know who you are!)

Nearly all of us have been caught in the quicksand that is YouTube, Reddit or Instagram, where you dip in a toe for a fleeting moment and get swallowed whole for an hour or more. And, gamers, come on! Two days straight of *World of Warcraft* or *SimCity* is unhealthy any way you cut it. Let's all admit that these time-wasters are fun and fascinating and, one could argue, not a complete waste of time despite the misnomer (look it up).

So, let's embrace 'em, but master them by knowing ourselves, having a plan, and assuming no one else cares if we sink into the depths of oblivion that is that game of *RISK* down the hall or the *Star Wars* marathon.

HERE ARE SOME TIPS:

- **Embrace 'em by actually treating yourself to a well-controlled amount.** For example, maybe after a rough day of class and studying, you'll treat yourself to an hour of YouTube gazing.

- **Have an alarm system and stick to it.** It's a little contract with yourself. BEFORE you sit down to do an hour of Facebook, actually set your cell phone alarm for that hour. When it goes off, jump up, log off, walk (or run) away from your computer, then turn off your alarm. YES, in that order!!!

- **Use strategies so you won't violate this little contract.** You might be saying to yourself that it's not that easy to walk away from Facebook. Your friends find you and start 'messaging' (ugh, a verb?!) you, and you can't help but talk to them. If so, then when you log into Facebook, try answering all your messages first BEFORE surfing around, so that little Facebook 'chore' will be done at the beginning. Also, when someone 'pings' you to chat as your 1-hour deadline is rapidly approaching, preface your response to them with, "Hey, great to hear from you, but I've gotta go soon... How ya doin'?" Then, when your alarm goes off, you've already primed them to know you would be leaving. Brilliant!!

- **Acknowledge what everyone already knows: if you've got your laptop and cell phone, you can bring any distraction with you.** So, now that we all know this, what's your plan? Try shutting them off and putting them out of site for 1-hour blocks. Then treat yourself to some texting during short study breaks, and treat yourself to Facebook or YouTube as an after-dinner break. (Remember, research suggests that looking at screens right before bed is bad for the brain, so pick a time that isn't just 'curling up in bed' with your laptop right before lights out.)

- **Single-Tasking Doesn't Suck & Multi-tasking is anathema (look it up!) to deep understanding.** There's emerging research suggesting that college students BELIEVE they are much better multi-taskers than they really are, and they're harming themselves without really knowing it. They think they're accomplishing more, but due to constant interruptions and battles for their attention, it's actually taking them longer to accomplish what they need to, and the quality of their end results is diminished. Huh... Who'd a thunk it? (Look it up!)

So, try single-tasking. All the cool (successful) kids are doing it.

Here's a quick story to close. One senior student I know told my class full of first-year students that he NEVER works on the weekends. He simply plays. They were both astounded and curious to know how he did it. Well, he explained that he treated Monday through Friday like a work week with full days 'at the office.' He got up early, worked hard during breaks between classes, stayed on campus instead of going home during the day, and limited his distractions. He planned well. He managed his time well. He worked hard and played hard.

He didn't waste time.

HOMESICK MY ASS!!

(aka Don't Be Such a Wuss!)*

"Be it ever so humble, there's no place like home."
— JOHN HOWARD PAYNE

Whenever he threw a big test at us, one of my high school teachers would always chuckle and bellow, "Gird your loins, my friends!" He meant that we should get ready for a battle (at least, I hope that's what he meant).

If ever there were something to battle through during your first semester at college, it's homesickness. Nearly everyone will encounter it in some way shape or form, and this battle is an important one to wage -- for your short-term survival and your long-term growth. Homesickness is simply a natural reaction to the newness of it all. New place. New people. New rules.

---

* Yes, I'm checking myself in for sensitivity training because of this chapter title.

New demands. When it reaches the point of sensory overload, which is highly probable, you're really just experiencing a desire for what is familiar and comfortable. If you 'give in' and run home too early for a quick fix of home-cooking and mommy time, it not only undercuts the independence you envisioned for yourself after high school, but it also sets a precarious stage for ongoing struggles back on campus. There are so many things to see and people to meet and activities to enjoy in the first month on campus, you don't want to miss them. More important, however, are the bonds that are being forged among new friends and dorm mates. If you miss these opportunities in the early weeks, it becomes MUCH tougher to cultivate social inroads later.

Call it weaning off of your parents. Call it 'cutting the cord.' But call it essential to your success. Here are some tips:

Do NOT even think about going home during the first month of school!! Stay on campus. If you forgot something from home, have it shipped. If your 'back home' friends want to see you, tell 'em you can video chat until they're willing to come visit you.

If there's a high school homecoming, plan for that to be your first visit back home (only if you want to and if you can). It will give you something about home to look forward to. You can see family and old friends in one fell swoop, have your fun, enjoy your old bed, get your fix, and get back to your new college home reinvigorated (except for the lost sleep from staying up too late and road-tripping). But let's be clear.… There ain't nothing wrong with staying on campus. Thanksgiving and winter breaks will be here sooner than you think.

21st Century technology makes the weaning process all too easy (or difficult if you're trying to shed your parents, but they keep Skyping you). Use these technologies to your advantage to give you a taste of home without going there. With cell phones and texting and video chat and Facebook, you can feel like you haven't left home anyway. Use them judiciously, however, because too much reliance on 'checking in with the homefront' might mean you'll never cut the cord.

Consider setting aside one hour per week to talk to your family and friends. Video chat might be best in terms of feeling 'real' and more personal (unless, of course, you don't want your folks to see what's behind your head on that dorm room wall). You can knock off a Skype to the family and a full Facebook session to check on high school friends in one hour easily. Then put it aside and get back to the business of books and your newfound social freedoms.

Who's in control? If you fall into the habit of leaving open the lifeline of text messaging and Facebook, continually interrupting you when 'they' see fit rather than when you see fit, the technology will control you rather than the other way around (and you might as well just be back home if you're going to be that connected). Soon you'll look up and wonder why you don't seem to be getting much studying done, or you can't comprehend and retain much of what you are 'learning'. Constant interruptions leave no room for depth of thought, internalization, or understanding. (When will you young whippersnappers figure this out?!) And they might even lead to bad feelings toward those people doing the interrupting.

Controlling Collisions. So... If you set aside chunks of time – an hour here and an hour there each week – to talk to your family and friends back home, you won't feel badly about shutting off your phone and Facebook when you're trying to study. The result will be that BOTH experiences will emerge as better quality experiences because you can devote yourself entirely to them and be present. If you allow those two worlds to continually collide, there will be damage. You will feel as though neither is of quality, which will create disappointment and stress. It's preventable if you choose to do so. (More on this later.)

Try writing a letter. That's right, a handwritten letter. Send one home, and you'll get one back. It's a real pick-me-up when you're off at school, and grandparents are really good at this, so keep them in the loop. (We'll talk more about grandparents in the upcoming 'Fonts of Wisdom' section.)

As you transition into college, a symbolic and literal shift into adulthood, your grandparents and parents will begin to treat you more like an adult. You'd be surprised how many stories they've been holding back and are just dying to tell you! Now's the time to move your communication into a new 'adult' phase, and a great way to open that communication is through a handwritten letter.

Do you know of your mom and dad's first date? Do you know of their first loves? How about your grandparents? What was their first big experience away from home? What was their first big purchase? Any big mistakes?

Take the time to write a letter to your parents and older relatives. Then, when you're feeling a bit homesick, that wonderful return letter will arrive and pick you right up. AND, you'll have some wonderful new insights into your older loved ones that you can retain forever and pass along to your kids someday.

This is what we call a 'Win–Win' scenario. Make it happen and help yourself in the process.

THE GREAT DEPRESSION

(aka Down in the Dumps)

"It doesn't hurt to feel sad from time to time."
— WILLY NELSON

There will be a time when you're away at college, and you will feel a bit down in the dumps, a bit sad, a bit melancholy. This will happen, even to the most well-adjusted, confident people. Know that it will come, embrace it, and plan for it.

The best preparation is to recognize that, for most people, a little bout of melancholy is brief and fleeting, and it will pass as quickly as it arrived. This recognition will help you embrace it when it comes and simply go with the flow – that is, try not to fight it too hard, which might make it worse and more prolonged. Next, have a little 'safe something' at the ready that can serve as a pick-me-up when sadness sets in. This can be treating yourself to a favorite book or movie, a trinket from home, or a rare and special snack (mine would be Chicago Style pizza shipped on dry ice from Lou Malnatti's pizzeria in Chicago – look it up). It could be running or working out, watching blooper footage of an old TV show on YouTube, or a special Skype session with your younger brother. Anything, essentially, that will make you smile just a smidge and help counterbalance your melancholy. Remember, you're not trying to fight it so much as to embrace it and soften the blow. So, make a list of these 'safe somethings' and tuck it away. When you need 'em, pull out the list and enjoy.

If it's a rare case, and your sadness doesn't subside, most campus counseling centers are top notch and ready to help. Plus, as with many resources, your tuition dollars are already paying for it, so why not use it?!

Sometimes, the walk over there in the fresh air may be all you'll need.

Carpe College

FONTS OF WISDOM

"When an old man dies, a library burns to the ground."
— AFRICAN PROVERB

"I like to listen.
I have learned a great deal from listening carefully.
Most people never listen."
— ERNEST HEMINGWAY

As you embark on this wonderful new chapter in your life, one of the greatest gifts you can give yourself is the willingness to fine-tune your listening skills. Remember the discussion about high school making you passive? Well, between your parents and your teachers, you've had lots of adults firing lots of advice your way for the past eighteen years or so. It's probably been coming at a rapid-fire clip lately as they all feel you slipping away from them and into adulthood. Your natural tendency, therefore, may have been to tune it all out or only give it a passive listen. In the short-term, that may have been a necessity. However, in the long-term, or even the not-too-distant term, it would be a big mistake.

It's time to start listening, really listening, again!

HISTORY MEETS THE HOMESICK BLUES

One of my favorite assignments for my high school students was an oral history project in which they were to talk to a family member from a previous generation (parents, grandparents, etc.), learn a family story, write down the story to submit to me, and present the story in front of class (orally from memory). What I loved about this project was several fold: it helped my students practice the communication skills we English teachers like; it got some of them talking to their parents and grandparents with new perspectives all around; and it secured for them family stories, pieces of their family history, that would be ingrained in their memories to hold forever and pass along to their own offspring.

Moreover, I got some vicarious satisfaction from it because my dad died when I was a sophomore in college, just as I was emerging as a young adult, and I missed out on myriad stories and conversations I wished he and I would have had. It was great to see these kids securing their own stories to more tightly weave their familial fabric.

As someone who's seen the value in the sharing of stories, and as someone who's felt the void in not securing those stories when I had the chance, I see the college years as presenting a critical opportunity for all parties to partake in a bit of family oral tradition. As I mentioned previously in that bit about writing letters, for many young people, the adults in their families have been shielding them from some of the 'juicier' stories, waiting until they might be old enough to understand. For some wonderful reason, when they head off to college many young people tend to cross over into the 'adult' realm in the eyes of their parents and grandparents. The maturation and distance seem to infuse everyone with a sense of being able to handle it, and the stories tend to leak out passively at family gatherings.

In my case, I remember realizing the relationship shifting during winter break of my college sophomore year. My dad picked me up after my return flight from the Rose Bowl game and took me for my first beer (i.e. the first time HE bought me one, not my first). We chatted for about an hour, the conversation peppered mostly with his questions about my trip, but what I remember most was the way he was treating me like a full-fledged adult. I could feel that positive shift in our relationship, and it made me happy.

He died a little over two months later. Not nearly enough time for this fledgling adult to tap into what he had to offer. So, when I said the stories 'leak' out passively, that was exactly how it happened in my experience. And, looking back, I think it was too slow, too passive, and clearly too late for me to glean a multitude of great tales from my dad.

Here are some snippets of stories that leaked out from my 'elders' as I moved into adulthood:
- One of the few times my dad had to draw his weapon when he served as a Chicago cop was at a bar. He was off duty, and he happened upon a guy trying to hold up the bartender at the cash register. My dad

drew his weapon, drew a bead on the bad guy, and hollered, "Stop. Police!" But he said he was so scared that he may have actually said, "Stop. PLEASE!"

- My great-aunt, the one with the messy, deep red lipstick and shiny gold in her teeth, had alcohol problems.
- My grandfather, a WWI German soldier, arrived in this country from Germany in the 1920s and painted churches until he could earn enough money to bring my grandmother over. They later had a son, my father, who fought for the U.S. in the second world war.
- My great uncle, a beat reporter for The Associated Press, met the police at a brothel raid during Prohibition, leaned against what was discovered to be a fake wall, and went crashing through it only to land on the lap of a patron, also a member of the police force.

These are all great and interesting stories to learn about one's family, but the problem here is in the 'leaking.' I waited passively until I stumbled upon the stories, or they simply seeped out at a family gathering when an elder forgot that they hadn't told the story in a while, and the next generation just happened to be in the right place at the right time to hear them. Otherwise, they may have gone unspoken or unheard.

So, my advice to you as you head off to college and into adulthood is to seek out the stories *actively* and *intentionally*. Tease them out. Leverage that shift in your relationship with the adults in your family and actively pursue what they have to offer. Set up time each week to chat with your folks and grandparents, but don't just tell them about your college life. Plan to ask them about their lives, too. Consider what you don't know, and start there. Who was your grandmother's first boyfriend? Did your grandfather serve in a war, and what was that like? What was your dad's first job? Did your mom ever break a boy's heart? How did your crazy uncle ever make millions off his invention?

This will be rich stuff that you won't want to miss. Sure, there will be some unsolicited advice thrown in, but the African proverb mentioned above, and my experience with my own father, aptly captures how important that sharing really is.

It's all wisdom, and it's all wonderful.

WISDOM COMES FROM FAR AND WIDE

Extending this listening theme further, heading off to college is a great time to re-think how you listen and the value of listening. Just think about all the great wisdom that will be around you all the time. Your peers from all parts of the world and all the wonderful perspectives they bring. Your professors. Your parents. Truly, from here on out, it would be wise to listen to anyone and everyone who has something to share. They are ALL fonts of wisdom or, at the very least, an inroad to an insight. So, consider each encounter with each person a learning opportunity.

Don't ignore a good idea just because it came from your parents, or from that professor you don't really care for. Yes, this is YOUR adventure and YOU want to do it on YOUR own! That goes without saying, and it truly is yours. However, as mentioned earlier, you do not sacrifice your independence by asking for help. Likewise, you do not sacrifice your independence because you chose to acknowledge that your parents had a good idea. It was just one good idea out of many to choose from, and YOU chose it. Who cares where the good idea came from? Making wise choices is the path you should take regardless of the idea's origins… that's just being smart.

Accepting wisdom, regardless of its source, is one of the toughest challenges for most independent-minded college students. Do you need to agree with everything anyone says? Of course, not. But respect all people and ideas publicly. Analyze and critique them privately. And accept wisdom when it rears its pretty head. This approach will contribute greatly to your continued development.

And you can start at your graduation party with your lovely aunt who's not afraid to tell you what's on her mind.

MOUTH BACTERIA MAKE YOU FART, SHEEP HAVE SOULS, AND FREE RANGE TURKEYS ARE FAT FREE*

(aka If Your Mother Says She Loves You, Check It Out)

Our previous chapter suggested that listening to everyone to glean new wisdom and insight is a good practice. And it is. But, as with most suggestions, there's a caveat. You're going to hear a lot of fascinating claims from a lot of dorm mates and classmates at college (not to mention some off-hand claims by your professors, too). This can serve as a great education provided by interesting people who hail from all over the globe, literally and figuratively. It's an intensely intellectual and mind-expanding environment, and everyone's going to be excited to share wise tidbits, trivia, and 'stuff I heard.' So, as an independent, self-directed learner, you need to have your radar up to detect when something is B.S. or brilliant or both.

Here's one way to think about it. Everyone has wisdom to share, from the best bathroom stalls to hangover cures to the hippest U.S. presidents, but you don't have to believe it just because they say it. Employ that old Russian proverb 'sampled' by Ronald Reagan: "Trust, but verify." It means you'd like to take somebody's word for it, but you're going to double check it anyway. Or you could go to the supreme extreme and use the old journalism warning, "If your mother says she loves you, check it out." Both are helpful approaches reminding us all to be careful with claims and to be sure nobody's

---

* I made up one of these claims in the title, but the other two claims have been posited out in the world already. Have fun figuring out which is which.

pulling the wool over our eyes (especially those soulful sheep mentioned in the title).

When overwhelmed by information, the risk is that you may be tempted to take shortcuts, jump to conclusions, rely on stereotypes, or just take somebody's word for it. Back when we talked about 'cultural screw-ups,' I suggested making a list and checking things out, so you could 'correct' stuff you may have misunderstood. Well, that same principle applies here, though it's not about turning the microscope on yourself; it's turning the microscope on the information you get from others. Think about sources. Where did that information come from? Whom should you trust for quality info about the dorms, your RA or that guy in your yoga class? Whom should you trust about STDs, the campus health center or that email that's been passed through 324 people? Whom should you trust for an opinion about that Physics professor, those who got D's or those who got A's?

Be a sponge, but be a filter, too. Treat everything you hear as fascinating wisdom with the potential for truth, but assume it was passed along through gossip, and question it accordingly.

Trust, but verify.

Now, go check out that story about your school's library sinking because the architects didn't take into account the weight of books in their initial designs and planning. As my grandma used to say, "Hogwash!"

If it helps to have a few go-to resources for bull★★★★ basics, try these:

Snopes.com
Skeptic.com
Urbanlegends.about.com
Randi.org
Factcheck.org
washingtonpost.com/blogs/fact-checker/

IF YOU'RE COCKY
AND YOU KNOW IT,
CLAP YOUR HANDS!

(aka, "So, You Didn't Have Your S★★★ Together the Way You Thought You Did, and Other Surprises That Really Suck")

Many first-year college students get blind-sided by something they didn't see coming. This is perfectly understandable because you have a lot on your plates. But by knowing yourself, having a plan, and assuming no one else cares, you can head off some unpleasant surprises. Let's look at some of these surprises and some, hopefully helpful, solutions.

HUMILITY VS. HUBRIS

When I use the word 'cocky' in this chapter's title or lob a loosely-worded assault like "You Didn't Have Your S★★★ Together," I know it's a bit obnoxious. But I'm trying to get your attention. And there is one particular time during your first year that seems to get everyone's attention: the day you get your first term's grades.

First semester grades come electronically right after students arrive home for winter break (on a quarter system, this might happen over the Thanksgiving holiday). Anticipating those first-term grades is an experience laden with excitement and trepidation, so many students tuck themselves away in some private little place and click the computer link for the grades that will give them their first official indication of how this college thing is REALLY going. For some, the results are not pretty, and they are disappointed. This disappointment stems, primarily, from a perceptual breakdown that might sound like this: "I thought I had a handle on my academics, but I guess I didn't." Enjoying newfound independence causes many new college students to believe they can simply do what they've always done and still crank out good grades. And it's a real blow to the ego when it doesn't turn out as expected.

This can be a very difficult time for you as a first-year student, but it's perfectly understandable how it can happen. First, as much as you might try to 'know thyself,' you can't possibly anticipate how you will react to every new college experience or how you will perform when faced with every new academic challenge. You're continually evolving, and these college years will probably bring more 'evolution' than you've ever experienced in your life so far. How you eat, sleep and live. How you think and what you believe. All of this is changing, and sometimes at a rapid pace. Every day you're encountering new relationships, new people and new ideas, and you're engaged in a continual examination of what it all means and where and how you fit in relation to it all.

Second, you are in entirely new surroundings, so whatever worked in past environments (e.g. high school) may not work in your new college environment. Given all the nuances, the people and places and ideas and perspectives, it's likely you will NOT have 'figured it all out' by the end of your first semester or even your first year. Also, it's highly likely you won't perform perfectly much of the time.

But if hubris gets in your way, you could have problems. Hubris is a false sense of confidence or an overestimation of one's capabilities. (If you want some good examples, revisit Odysseus in Homer's *The Odyssey* — Look it up!) Many first-year students exhibit hubris on at least a few occasions, thinking you know it all or have a firm grasp on how it all works. Again, it is perfectly understandable as you try to independently and confidently find your way. But it's also very important to recognize when your perceptions are off and you don't know it all. Those who do not reflect on these occasions and make appropriate adjustments tend to crash and burn. Those who exhibit some humility, on the other hand, by keeping an open mind and recognizing that they still have much to learn, tend to find success quicker.

As you navigate your first year confidently believing you have your act together and that your way is the best way, it might be a good idea to keep Oliver Cromwell's admonition in mind: "I beseech you... think it possible you may be mistaken."

So, when you have these moments of awakening, these blows to your ego, like being mistaken, or disappointed and surprised by your first round of grades, you can use them as an opportunity to reflect and to set things right. And there's no better time for reflection than during that holiday break right after the grades arrive. Try this....

WINTER BREAK BREAKTHROUGHS

Come home for winter break, enjoy seeing your family and friends again, celebrate the holidays.... Do all of these fun things, of course. But also remember that the holidays are a great time for rest and reflection, and this is never more true than for the first-year college kid during winter break. So, have some fun and get some rest, but then be sure to carve out some time to reflect on how the first semester went. Consider these reflective questions:

- Was the first semester just how I'd envisioned it? If not, why not?
- What were the good, the bad, and the ugly parts?
- Were there courses where I expected to do better? Which ones? What broke down?
- Were there courses I knew would be hard, but I tried to tackle them alone, and I should have sought help earlier?
- Were there courses where I knew I could have done better, but I dropped the ball and didn't work hard enough?
- Were there courses or professors that left me uninspired and unmotivated, and I just didn't invest myself as a result?
- Was my overall academic approach a sound one, or does it need some adjusting? What adjustments should there be? (For ideas, look back at the earlier "Have a Plan" section.)
- What about my relationships? Are my roommate and I cool, or do we need to communicate better? Do I know enough people from my dorm, and am I happy with those relationships? What about relationships with classmates? Do I know at least one person from every class? Could I?
- What about activities and clubs? Did I try enough? Did I miss out on anything I'd like to try now? Did I look at all the offerings at the beginning of the year, but then get in a rut and forget about these options? Why not try something new next semester?

The purpose of all this reflection is to continue to try to 'know thyself' a bit better, given this new phase of your life, and to start building a new plan for success. Consider this: your college experience is going to last about four years (give or take). If you fumble and stumble your way through all of it, you won't be that attractive to potential employers, potential grad schools, or even potential mates in the end. But if you fumble and stumble early on, you reflect on those experiences and build an improvement plan, and then you actually show improvement after that initial rocky start, you'll have an easy story to tell (and to 'sell') to any interested parties.

Did somebody say PARTY?! Wooooooo..........

SOME MORE SNEAKY SURPRISES

These have nothing to do with being cocky or careless, it's just that students always seem to be surprised by a couple of other doozies: Course and Housing Registration.

Over the summer, before you arrive on campus, there are a whole lot of people making sure that you have your residence hall housing in order and that you've got your course schedule all ready to go. You'll receive notices from your college, and your parents will have given you a near third-degree burn from breathing down your neck to make sure you've got all your ducks in a row. While it seems like overkill, in the end you'll be happy to have that kind of attention.

After the school year begins, however, the deadlines for enrollment in second semester courses and signing up for housing selection for your second year always seem to spring out of nowhere. And they always seem to surface when you're swamped with school work for your current classes. Sure, there will be a few notices from your academic advisor and the housing folks, but these could get lost in the shuffle, AND there's some important planning you'll have to do to create the best outcome for yourself.

Your course schedule and your living arrangements will be, arguably, the most significant aspects of your college life moving forward. Imagine if you've got a four-hour night class one night, and an 8am class the next day. Imagine if it's with a professor everyone says is a poor teacher. Imagine having a long day, followed by a 30-minute bus ride to your off-campus apartment, another hour to cook your own meal, and a set of new roommates lounging around that you don't really care for. These are all real possibilities if you don't plan well, and ironing out the details is supremely important. But just knowing the deadlines is not enough.

Here are some tips for your second round of course registration:

- Review your notes from your fall registration. Presumably, you sat with your parents, an older sibling, a college rep or your college course registration guide to give you an overview of the course sequence for first-year students and your selection options. (If you are a first-generation college student, I hope your college reached out to assist you, or you found a helpful high school counselor for guidance.)

In any case, revisit what you did to prepare for your fall course enrollment, review which choices went well and which did not, and factor that into your planning for second semester. In many cases, the core requirements for the entire first year are pretty clear-cut, and you may only have to (get to?) select a few electives.

- Check your college academic calendar to see when course registration begins for second semester (and for your second year), and mark those dates in your personal planner. Then pick another date one month prior to that, and mark your personal planner with a reminder to contact your academic advisor. While they may be contacting you, they're busy people, so be an advocate for yourself. Contact your advisor on that date to schedule a face-to-face meeting to discuss your future course selection.

- Don't forget about other resources. Remember that knowledge is power. Talk to professors and peers and upperclassmen students who might have great insights about whether the courses you're planning to take are right for you or for your learning style. Have conversations with these people about your plans and keep an open mind to their insights.

- Remember that in some course registration systems, first-year students have a lower priority for scheduling, and you may not get your preferred choices. Even with all your great advanced planning, you may not get what you want. So, be prepared with 'decent' and 'acceptable' plans B, C, and D if your first choices fall by the wayside.

Here are some tips for planning your living arrangements for your second year:

- Just like course registration, advanced planning will help. In fact, your courses might end up being even easier to plan than your housing will be. Reviewing what you did in the fall will be helpful, but on many campuses, your choices for your second year become much more broad. You might be able to move out of the residence halls and into an apartment. That apartment may be on campus, or you could move off campus. Your lease may be through your college, or it may be through a private landlord. Instead of being assigned a roommate or choosing just one, you may get to select several roommates.

   While reviewing your notes from the fall is a good start, you should also visit your campus housing website, and you should schedule a meeting with someone from your housing office.

- Find the housing enrollment deadline on your campus calendar and put that date into your personal planner. Pick a date one month prior, and schedule a meeting with a housing representative.

- Prior to meeting with a housing rep, do some personal research and reflection so you have an idea of what your own criteria will be for choosing housing for your second year. Consider these questions to begin:

  - Do you like your current roommate?
  - Do you like your current cafeteria food?
  - Do you like your walk to class?
  - Do you like the convenience of your laundry facilities?
  - Would you like to experiment with apartment living?
  - Have you ever prepared your own meals consistently?
  - Could you live in an apartment and still keep a campus dining plan?
  - Would you need special transportation if you moved into an apartment?
  - What are the cost factors comparing residence halls to other living arrangements?
  - Could you find furniture if you moved to an unfurnished apartment or house?
  - Do you have anyone in mind you'd like to live with?
  - How well do you know their living habits?
  - Is there anyone you would refuse to live with if they surprised you and asked you?
  - How many roommates do you think you could handle?

If you have thought about these matters before meeting with a housing rep, you should be in great shape. Yes, there will still be some things that are outside your control, but with decent planning you'll be in much better shape.

★★★

NOTE: The real surprises begin after winter break when some students have a good idea of whom they'd like to ask to be roommates for next year, and other students are not quite prepared or haven't given it much thought. So, you get some lovely scenarios playing out all over the dorms, like people saying "Yes, I'll room with you next year," even though they don't want to, but they were caught off guard. Or some current dorm mates teaming up with a plan to live together in an apartment, but one gets left behind because there's not enough space. A whole slew of communication and emotional issues can surface when you're talking about this important part of your lifestyle.

Getting your house in order, so to speak, makes every other aspect of your life easier. If you don't want to be worrying about roommates or bus routes or grocery store visits or household chores or meal planning while you're trying to do well in school, then get your act together ahead of time.

Remember? Know thyself. Have a Plan. Assume no one else cares…. Blah, blah, blah…

Carpe College

ADVOCATE & ACT

(Quickly & Decisively)

"Action expresses priorities."
— MOHANDAS GANDHI

Just as you take action to ensure your physical and mental health (which we'll address in the next chapter), it's important to take action to ensure that you're defending all of your needs and values. Think of it like this: ALL students are special needs students. Your needs are unique and special, just as important as every other student, and you shouldn't be shy about it. Since 'no one else cares,' you should be your own best advocate in every dimension of your life, from academics to the rest.

KEEP YOUR GOALS FRONT & CENTER

Every one of your peers has his or her own goals and motivations. Keep yours at the forefront. If people start tailgating for the football game at 9am but the game doesn't start until 1pm, it's okay to hit the library until 11:00 and show up to the tailgate a bit late. Trust me, the people running the keg don't care how you do on your tests next week!

SPEAK UP!

If you don't understand something, SAY SO! Ask questions. Do NOT waste time fumbling and stumbling and not knowing something. Ask the professor, ask your peers, ask a tutor, try YouTube or other online resources.

Remember the 'pebble in the pond' approach. Those closest to you, your peers, typically have some of the best information on who the best professors are, where the best food is, how to find the best phone apps or the best off-campus apartment for next year. ASK. ASK. ASK.

HELP THEM HELP YOU

I do not like retail stores. I do not browse. If I need a new pair of jeans, I enter the store, head directly to a sales associate, and ask for help. I let them get me to the jeans section, show me my options, and then I turn 'em loose. They are there to help, and I let them help. I like libraries, but if I'm on a research mission, I do not browse. I enter a library and head straight for a librarian. I ask a question. They answer and guide me to where I need to be. They are there to help, and I let them help.

I do NOT spend time wandering around wondering why they may have moved the jeans aisle or why there are four new DVD sections where the non-fiction used to be. I let them help me.

Consider this approach for most aspects of your college campus life… at least while you're learning the ropes. It's about productivity overall, but the two key elements to consider are (1) helping yourself, and (2) time. To reach your goals you need to be productive. To accomplish that, you need to effectively manage the resources around you. And, to do that, you need to do it efficiently (i.e. in a timely manner). Remember that lots of students have come before you, and 'the experts' have figured out what most students need and put those resources in place. Then they CHARGED STUDENTS MONEY (i.e. tuition) to make them available to students.

The resources (including people to answer your questions) are there to help you. If you do not reach out to them, however, they cannot help. And, again, your tuition has already paid for it.

NET RESULTS

When considering your quest to achieve your goals, the role college plays, the obstacles you may encounter, and the assistance you may need from others, please don't forget this: THEY WANT YOUR MONEY!! They have put resources in place to help you battle through challenges and keep you in school. Think about it. You stay, you pay! If you fail and drop out, that's a lose-lose scenario for all involved. So, there are 'safety nets' in place in every aspect of the campus experience to help you remain there. Whether it's study skills, timely tutoring or housing help, the resources are in place.

Yes, they have your money, and although they may not be laughing all the way to the bank, they're certainly smiling a bit wider because of it. However, if you fully utilize the available resources designed to assist you,

you'll get to smile a little wider, too. And you'll feel like you got your money's worth in the end.

BUT YOU MUST SPEAK UP AND ASK!!

MIND & BODY:
THE DYNAMIC DUO

"A strong body makes the strong mind."

— THOMAS JEFFERSON

Take care of your body, or you'll screw up your mind. It's that simple! This is nothing new, and there's plenty of empirical evidence out there to support it, but really it's just common sense and stands to reason. Just think back to your previous schooling. If you were too tired or hungry or felt a little under the weather, it was very hard to concentrate on school stuff. That will only be exacerbated at the college level.

Think about it. You're heading off to a new environment where you will encounter people from all over the globe, and you're going to be packed into tight living spaces, dormitories and classrooms, '24/7' (as the kids used to say). There's not a chance that you will have built up immunities to every virus your fellow students might have, and vice-versa. Coming and going in and out of all those buildings and bathrooms and classrooms and cafeterias, there's not a chance you can avoid getting exposed to some nasty stuff. So, the best defense is a good offense. 'An ounce of prevention is worth a pound of cure,' as Ben Franklin so wisely put it. You've got to get your body as healthy as possible to ward off the tough stuff to come.

Why bother? Well, let's revisit that tried and true formula about spending two hours outside the classroom for every one hour in. Imagine that you catch some bug and fall ill for two days. Imagine that you miss classes on Monday and Tuesday as a result, totaling seven hours over those two days. You also just lost fourteen hours of prep/study time. Now it's Wednesday, you're heading back to class, but you're playing catch up. If you had your act together, you emailed your professors to tell them of your illness, and you got an overview of what you missed. If not, you're even farther behind because now you have to circle back around to meet with them and get up to speed.

Where are you going to add in those fourteen hours you lost? How are you going to catch up? It's doable, but it's not easy.

The train just keeps moving, and you're trying to catch it (AND get your strength back from being under the weather).

There is a better way:

EXERCISE REGULARLY

We already talked about how frequently college kids are working out. It's now the norm. Those campus facilities are pretty darn nice most of the time. Just join the crowd, build it into your regular schedule, and feel better. Try it before a class and see if the research is correct: you are more alert and receptive to learning after exercise! Plus, most campuses have some sort of wellness program, so you might find a nutritionist or trainer to help you establish your fitness plan for free. Wow! One more thing your tuition already paid for.

EAT WELL

Nutritionist or not, your college cafeteria (or food court, or gourmet eatery, or whatever wonderful amenity you kids get nowadays) will have plenty of healthy food offerings. There will surely be fruits and veggies, and you should simply plan to partake of them. Eat some fruits or veggies at each meal. Pick the ones you like (or can tolerate), and eat 'em FIRST when you're most hungry. Then they're out of the way, you can move on to dessert or whatever order you wish, and you'll have a healthy balance with all the great vitamins and nutrients fresh produce provides.

Research suggests that 'grazing' (eating smaller amounts more frequently throughout the day) may be the healthiest approach to eating. Dr. Bill Sears suggests his Rule of Twos: eat twice as often, eat half as much, and chew twice as long. Some college cafeterias and meal plans accommodate and encourage this approach. That is, they let you eat as frequently as you wish. (They don't really care how you chew!) So, you can bop in to grab something small between classes and not be charged for a full meal. Regardless of what your meal plan allows, a banana, orange, or energy bar between classes is not a bad call any way you slice it (or peel it).

GET SERIOUS ABOUT SLEEP

College life will, no doubt, challenge your concepts and habits of sleep. Your course schedule or your social schedule may not fit your biological clock. You will be in a new bed in a new room in new surroundings, and the people around you may make more noise than you're used to. Your mind is going to be challenged (by academic and non-academic demands) like it's never been challenged before, and you WILL get tired.

Know this. Plan for this.

The research is about as varied and scattered as a crazy REM-cycle dream after a spicy bowl of chili. Most data suggest we all need about eight hours of sleep each night, but few of us get it. If you can get it in one chunk, that seems to be best, but some evidence suggests that small chunks of sleep, as long as it's deep sleep, can also be beneficial. Most evidence suggests that consistent sleep time from night to night is better than staggered. For example, getting to bed EACH night by midnight and sleeping until 7am is probably better than getting to bed by 9pm on Monday, then midnight on Tuesday, then 3am, then midnight, and so on. To complicate matters, short 'cat naps' seem to provide benefit, too. So if you can close your eyes for 15 minutes before class, you may feel rejuvenated and lucid. However, if you fall into a habit of taking three hour naps in between classes, that can really throw off your sleep patterns at night, making it harder for you to get to sleep at a reasonable hour and throwing you off for the next day and the next (not to mention missing three hours of productivity during the day – when most people are awake).

So, give some serious thought to PLANNING YOUR SLEEP PATTERN and trying to stick with it. If you falter, fill it in with short, catch-up naps (as long as you DON'T fall into the trap of sleeping during the day). This appears to be the healthiest approach.

LOSE THE LAPTOP

It's been your lifeline all day long. Don't take it to bed with you! New evidence suggests that electronic devices stimulate brain activity, making it harder to drift off to sleep. There's even some thinking that the bright screen light can disrupt the brain chemistry involved in your sleep cycle.

So, dim the screen light, and lose the electronic devices an hour before bedtime. Try curling up with a good book (of the non-electronic variety). You guys remember what books are, right?! You know, paper pages, binding that crackles when you open it.... Sound familiar?

REVIEW AND REVISIT

Review and revisit all that's been mentioned previously about working out sleep and alarm clock matters with your roommate. Also revisit the notion of putting EVERYTHING in your planner. What if your planner said you were to sleep from 11pm – 7am? Could you stick to it? Try it.

Your body and mind are the Dynamic Duo. Keep 'em strong!

LOOK!
I CAN SEE
YOUR BREADTH!

"Passions are the gales of life."

— ALEXANDER POPE

What do you want to be when you grow up?

Talk about pressure! You young people have been harangued and harassed without end about solidifying your future, locking something in, having a plan. Yet, ironically, you have grown up in a time when options are more vast and unpredictable than ever before, and you are (arguably) less prepared to make such choices than ever before.

THE TERRAIN

Think on this... When you were born, just under two decades ago, there was no Facebook or Google or YouTube or Twitter or iPhone or drone aircraft or flat TVs or hybrid cars. There were CDs and Blockbuster videos, but how quickly they came and went! That's the point – quickly. With technological advances, particularly in the way information is shared and the pace at which it is shared, new ideas and developments are emerging exponentially. And, on the heels of that, new career paths follow. You've been told that your generation will probably switch jobs (and careers) far more frequently than previous generations, and your choices are more varied than ever. On the other hand, you've had cursory career exploration assessments (of the standard, #2 pencil variety) since middle school, and you've had helicopter parents as recently as... well...maybe this morning. Most of your 'exploration' has consisted of organized, orchestrated, and adult-officiated activities, leaving scant opportunity for you to truly explore whether you like the science lab more than the music studio or the soccer field.

So, this is the zeitgeist (look it up). This is the landscape. Parents (and others) telling you to make up your mind, buckle down, and lock into a major that will garner you the most practical path to a career, but not enough experience to make a truly informed choice. You're not alone. Previous generations had similar decisions at your age. However, they've never had the variety of choices to complicate those decisions. Moreover, most honest educators will share our dirty little secret: We have very little idea about what careers will look like in the next couple of decades. Sure, we'll need doctors. Sure, computers will be involved. Sure, we'll always need accountants. (Prostitution? Sadly, there's one that seems to have some staying power.) But with the likes of Facebook and YouTube listed above, we've seen a landscape that can be altered significantly in a very short period. Consider how quickly 'mobile apps' emerged and how young people are building entire professional lives creating and marketing them. Consider the push for sustainability and LEED certification of new buildings and the career paths that has spawned. On the other hand, when was the last time you met a tobacco farmer or a travel agent or newspaper person or music label who hasn't had the rug pulled out from under them because… well… times change?

STEALING A STRATEGY FROM SCOUTING

This 'rug pulling' will probably continue at a quicker and more expanded clip in generations to come simply because changing technologies change what we need our humans to do and how they do it. Just think about what wonderful opportunities emerged from the invention of the printing press. How about the automobile? So, now we have the Internet. And, in your lifetime, we'll probably have something akin to vacations in space. Talk about cracking open the opportunities!

So, what does that mean for a young person embarking on a college career and a professional life? It means it's time to steal from the Boy Scouts again: Be Prepared!

I encourage students to take a look at a landscape where change – often, rapid change – can upend careers, and to follow this advice: ***Take a deep 'BREADTH.'*** Yes, it's a clever play on words to suggest that the more curiosity, interest and ability you have spread across differing domains, the better able you will be to land upright if you get bounced around. The more breadth of interest and experience you have, the less bouncy a career adjustment will feel. If you've prepared for a career, but technological advances make that career irrelevant, you will need to be able to find something new. So, be prepared by keeping all your passions and hobbies bubbling forth. That is, even though you may have chosen environmental engineering as your career path, it's okay and wise to stay involved with your theater group. Even though you want to be a math teacher, it's okay and wise to keep writing songs and playing guitar. Even though you want to be a financial analyst, it's okay and wise to keep making short films on the weekends. Don't get so locked into your major that you leave behind other aspects of your life.

You just never know when a rug might get pulled or a path might get altered and, five or ten or twenty years down the road, those passions might meld into your next career. Maybe you'll leave engineering to write plays about the environment. Maybe you'll be a great math teacher singing engaging songs you wrote to teach your students math. Maybe you'll make financial advice videos, get discovered, and become the next big online expert. Maybe you'll be like Steve Jobs, who took an entirely impractical calligraphy course in college only to have it pay off immensely ten years later as he developed the first Macintosh computer.

Harvard's guru on happiness, Daniel Gilbert, suggests that we humans have a terrible track record for predicting what might make us happy. Much of finding our bliss will be done through trial and error. That means we need to keep trying lots of different stuff: majors and careers and hobbies and interests. Since no one knows what the future holds, doesn't it make sense, now more than ever, to have many irons in the fire, many lines in the water, many passions bubbling forth?

Better safe than sorry. Plan ahead. Be prepared.

★★★

NOTE: This would also be the best place to advise against following the political pendulum swings or pressures to chase money by choosing a 'practical' major over the liberal arts. The pressures to go to college to 'be employable' are greater now than ever before. However, the reasoning behind this tactic is quite murky, and I encourage you to research the wonderful online discussions and debates that are emerging on this topic (and the long-term value of a liberal arts degree). You might also be interested in checking out what the Fortune 500 CEOs think about what matters for their incoming employees. Or, you might want to check out what majors those highly successful CEOs chose. Then talk to your folks and discuss amongst yourselves. I have a personal bias towards the liberal arts for fostering critical thought, reasoned arguments, cogent communications (especially writing), and the ability to synthesize myriad perspectives into a broader, more connected whole. So, why not go for that liberal arts major, and minor in something 'practical.' Or, do a double major, for goodness sake! Carpe College!

EXTRA EXERCISE: *Why not check in on some adults close to you? Pick any 10 adult family members or acquaintances, ask them these questions, and prepare to be enlightened.*

1. *What was your college major?*
2. *Why did you choose it?*
3. *Do you use it in your current profession, and to what extent?*
4. *What do you think would be a great double-major? Why?*
5. *If you could do college all over again, what if anything would you do differently?*
6. *Are you happy with your college experience and professional life overall?*

THINKING INSIDE
THE BOX

"Do not dwell in the past, do not dream of the future,
concentrate the mind on the present moment."

— BUDDHA

What follows is brief, but it just may be the most important approach in your *Carpe College!* philosophy. The ability to compartmentalize, to put something in a figurative box, focusing on that thing alone, and then to be able to set it aside when necessary, is a very important life skill, and it will enhance your college experience greatly.

When I was a kid, and we were doing weekend cleaning in my home, my dad would say in a repetitive and almost sing-song manner, "A place for everything, and everything in its place." It was a nice (annoying?) way to promote good organization, and he made the more important point that, if you knew where you kept something, you didn't need to spend a lot of mental energy on it. You didn't have to wonder where you left it or wonder if it's okay. When you needed your basketball shoes, you knew exactly where to find your basketball shoes.

At a broader level, I think this is a wonderful way to approach college. Consider all the thoughts, emotions, coursework, relationships, expectations and responsibilities that will be swirling around in your life. Wouldn't it be great if you could place each course in a box, each relationship in a box, and pull them out only when you're ready to devote yourself entirely to them? Not only would this make your life more organized and manageable, but it should also allow you to enjoy each and every experience as you are having it without distractions creeping in. When you pour yourself into your Econ essay, you can fully enjoy the effort, depth of thought, and learning that are a part of that immersion. When you're on the phone with your boyfriend, free of all other distractions, you can truly enjoy that moment.

It's like a daily quest to find joy and fascination in each and every experience. You're focusing on one thing at a time as you are doing it. You are single tasking, living in the moment, being present. Whether it's a lecture, a good dorm conversation, or a chat with your parents, focusing solely on the thing itself has the potential to make it great, to make it 'the best ever.'

Imagine each day filled with a bunch of 'best evers.' It's a good way to *Carpe College!* and a good way to launch life from here on out.

TEMPUS FUGIT

(More Latin?! You're Killing Me, Smalls!)

*"Life is all memory, except for the one present moment
that goes by you so quickly you hardly catch it going."*
— TENNESSEE WILLIAMS

*"A baby holds your hands, and then suddenly,
there's this man lifting you off the ground, and then he's gone.
Where is that son?"*
— ANDRE, *MY DINNER WITH ANDRE*

Time has flown, and we have reached the end of this book. It's only fitting, therefore, that we return to the concept of time because its management and fleeting nature are what cause the most consternation for most college students.

HIGH SCHOOL HAPPENED. EMBRACE THE PACE.

High school is already in your rear-view mirror. Just think about how quickly that happened. Wasn't it only a few eye blinks ago that you were cautiously entering those intimidating high school doors? Didn't it fly by at warp speed? Well, college will be the same. There will be so much that is new to you, so much processing of information, that you will become immersed in it and lose track of time. Then, like a friendly firefly, your college years will have illuminated and left as quickly as they came.

This is not a bad thing. It is a reality. Deep experiences cause us to forget time, and college WILL be a deep experience. And, you can only truly come to know this timelessness in the same way that you came to know it about high school – after the fact. Of course, in your day-to-day college life you'll have a schedule with places to go and people to see, and you'll retain your functional sense of time. But then, in a snap, it will be over, and it'll feel like it flew. Because it did.

A BROADER PLAN

The benefit of hearing this now, however, can help you recognize it for what it is and, as our mantra suggests, 'have a plan.' Since you are not yet immersed in it, this is a great time to build a broad plan. And by broad, I mean stuff like this:

- Embrace the absence of time. Ironically, if you plan well, you can allow yourself to get lost in moments where you won't need to think about time at all. Think about leaving yourself some of that time each week.
- As mentioned in 'Thinking Inside the Box,' try to truly savor the moments, large and small, as they are happening:
  - –when a professor is having an inspired and passionate moment and you see how much she loves her subject
  - –when you have an epiphany, realizing something new about yourself or the world
  - –when you see someone else grow
  - –when you don't hit it off with someone, and that's okay
  - –when you're doing something crazy, losing yourself in the moment
  - –when you realize you just accomplished something difficult, and you got through it on your own
  - –when you let a friend teach you something
  - –when a kiss is just a kiss
  - –when morning comes earlier than expected
  - –when things went bad but got better
  - –when the dorm discussion trails on past midnight
  - –when the student theater production is the perfect mix, showing signs of both learning and mastery
  - –when you helped someone
  - –when something your parents said years ago finally makes sense
- Try to remember that academics are paramount, but there must be more to it than that! Remember that, in the arc of your life, this

college thing is a phase, a tiny blip on the radar. An intense blip, but a blip nonetheless. A mere four years in an 80-plus year lifespan. It's a launching pad to something else. It is an opportunity to prepare for what's next. And there will be a whole lot of 'what's next' covering more than just book learning. So, in ALL aspects of your college life, explore and discover, explore and discover, explore and discover in the hope of being ready to launch the rest of your life and ask 'How high is up?'

To close, I'd like you to keep in mind a guiding thought. For this very short period of time in your life, and possibly never again, you will be given a very unique gift: a supremely rich environment with ample time, space, safety and people to explore whatever interests you intensely, to push yourself, to make mistakes and recover from them, and to live as deeply as you'd like in the hope of finding yourself or, at least, the beginnings of yourself.

Such an opportunity may never present itself again. So, embrace it and…

Carpe College!

Oh yeah! And don't forget the mantra:

Know thyself. Have a plan. Assume no one else cares.

Sorry. One more thing. Did I mention…?

Carpe College!

Appendices

APPENDIX A:
THE JUNE QUESTION (AND A FEW MORE)

In order to know what to do today and tomorrow, it's important to know where you're heading. You need direction. You need goals. You need finish lines. And that's what this whole "June Question" thing is all about.

If you recall from earlier reading, this question is going to come during the summer after your first year, whether you like it or not. Your friends and family are probably going to greet you with it as soon as they see you. "How was your first year?" they will holler exuberantly. And you had better be ready with an answer.

To ensure you have good answers, it's best to consider (and even write down) some of your thoughts about the June Question long before June arrives. Let's begin.

Next June, what do you want to say about your entire first year…

Regarding your grades?

Regarding your learning?

Regarding how much you LIKED your classes?

Regarding your relationships with professors?

Regarding your roommate?

Regarding new friends?

Regarding your life outside the classroom? (Bulletin Board Bingo, anyone?!)

Regarding your progress toward professional skill development (internships, job shadowing?)

Now use the rest of this blank page to chart HOW you're going to achieve all of this.

And if you're happy with this process, turn the June Question into the Graduation Question, and try to answer all these questions for four years from now.

APPENDIX B:
'DON'T HATE THE MATE' SHARE SHEET
(FOR SHARING WITH PROSPECTIVE ROOMMATES)

In our 'Don't Hate the Mate' chapter, we talked about how good communication is key to roommate relationships, and how that communication can, and should, begin BEFORE meeting in person in the fall. Knowing that you can't possibly predict your exact sleep schedule and social behaviors once you actually begin your 'dorm living,' the questions below will help you prevent some of the issues that could fester and grow.

Feel free to share this with your new roommate via social media, and maybe even do the exercise together. It's either going to help you start bonding right away, or scare the s★★★ out of you!

1. What smells bug you? (Body odor? Potpourri? Are you a fresh air freak where you'd rather have the window open in the winter time and wear a sweater than smell that thick, musty indoor air?)

2. What sounds bug you? (Screamo music? Only hearing one side of a phone conversation? Snoring? Alarm clock sounds? Toenail clipping?)

3. What sights bug you? (Messy spaces? Open curtains? Sunlight in the morning? Black-light posters? Cat posters? The color yellow? Old tennis shoes? Anything other than complete darkness when you sleep?)

4. What's your greatest fear or concern about your prospective roommate(s)? (He's a Taylor Swift fan? She will bring boys into our room for 'extra-curricular activities? He will play video games all day and never talk to me? She won't like it WHEN I borrow her clothes?)

5. What are you like when at your worst? (When upset, do you shut down? Do you rage for five minutes and then want to be buds again? Are you a little passive aggressive? Does it help if someone brings you ice cream?)

NOTE: If you have trouble coming up with answers to these questions, you are going to be an incredibly tolerant roommate, and anyone would be glad to share space with you.

Answer the questions honestly and share your responses with your prospective roommate(s). If Taylor Swift or black-light posters or borrowing clothes will be a deal-breaker, it is absolutely best to figure that out sooner rather than later. In fact, having reflected on these things that bug you, maybe this is a good time to consider if they REALLY are deal-breakers, or if, with a little bit of effort, they could fall within your expanded level of tolerance. If you think you could tolerate them, imagine doing so EVERY day for the ENTIRE school year. That should be a good indicator.

Again, know thyself.

APPENDIX C:
WEEKLY PLANNER SAMPLES

Some funny dude once exclaimed that your life at college is going to include three main elements: School, Sleep, and Fun, and you should pick two 'cause that's all you'll be able to have.

That is funny, and there is some wisdom buried there in terms of the kind of juggling you'll need to do. HOWEVER, *Carpe College!* says this is a crock of s★★★!

If you have a plan, you should be able to have your cake and eat your school, sleep and fun, too. Yes, sometimes schoolwork will demand more of your time. Yes, you'll do a late party a time or two. Yes, you'll sleep in on occasion. In any given week, these three elements may get out of whack. But over the long haul of the entire year, if you plan well, you'll be able to say you carpe'd it all and did so with quality and gusto.

The following pages include four sample student weekly plans, building from one that wants no school work on the weekends (Plan 1) to one that seems to find a way to pack in a ton of stuff (Plan 4). I've even tossed in a fifth plan to show what 'winging it' might look like (even though someone who's really winging it wouldn't use a plan at all). That one's a recipe for trouble, though, so use it for comparison purposes only.

Obviously, the classes, activities and other details in these plans will be different for you. These 'puzzle pieces' are always going to change from semester to semester. However, you should be able to mix and match and piece together a schedule that works for you.

Some things to note about these plans:
- They assume the formula: for every 1 hour in the classroom, study for 2 hours out.
- Four classes (a typical load) are represented: Statistics, Calculus, Economics and International Relations.
- The plans begin at 9am (after an hour of morning bathroom routine & breakfast) and end at 9pm. That's a 12-hour day, and once you start loading in some activities or some part-time work, those twelve hours are chock-full of stuff. It will seem like there's not much wiggle or breathing room when you get to the later plans. HOWEVER, the truth is, you can actually work harder. Imagine if your day didn't end at 9pm, but ended at 11pm Monday through Friday. You just added another 10 hours to your week, which could help you accomplish a whole lot more AND free up even more valuable weekend time.
- Sample Plan #1 begins with fewer demands on the student's time and

an eagerness to keep the weekends free. It's doable, but it's not really carpe-ing the most out of the collegiate week. You'll see plenty of white space on that weekend.

- Sample Plan #2 adds in a couple of weeknight activities, like Student Senate and Volleyball. That pushes some study time to the weekend, but still leaves plenty of room for sleeping and partying.
- Sample Plan #3 takes into account a part-time job along with all the other stuff, and you can see the balance of Sleep-School-Fun is stretched nearly to its limits.
- Sample Plan #4 includes all the aforementioned studying and activities, and then throws a Saturday football game into the works, bumping the part-time job to Sunday. THIS is the full extent of a Carpe College week. This student has decent studying time, a leadership activity (student senate), a social activity (volleyball), a part-time job, a religious activity, fitness, relaxing, and a bit of sleeping, eating and showering thrown in the mix. While this is NOT typical, you can see that it is achievable.

HOWEVER, if you choose to drink at a tailgate party before and/or after the game, you might enjoy your Saturday, but you might be pretty worthless trying to recover. And, given that the Stats & Calc study time got displaced and will have to be moved to after 9pm on other weeknights, you can't afford to be less than lucid when Monday rolls around.

★★★

NOTE: Drinking really can alter these plans because of recovery time. If you drink to excess one night, there's a lot of recovery time the next day, and that can throw off your entire plan for the week. If you drink in moderation, there's less recovery time and a better chance to stick to your plan. If you don't drink at all, which, believe it or not, is true for many college students, you'll get good sleep with no wasted recovery time the next day. (Plus, alcohol involves a lot of empty calories you'd be adding to your normal intake, almost guaranteeing you gain those 'freshmen fifteen' pounds. If you want to shed them, that'll take more time. Just something to think about as you plan.)

★★★

So, take a peek at the following plans and see which one might work for you (HINT: I'm hoping its not Sample Plan #5, which isn't really a plan at all).

WEEKLY PLANNER 1: Weekends Free

(CLASSES SHOWN IN BOLD: Statistics, International Relations, Economics, Calculus)

	8am	9	10	11	12	1pm	2	3	4	5	6	7	8	9
M	B&B* *Bathroom Routine & Breakfast	IR Study	IR Study	IR Study	**Intl. Relations**	Lunch	**Econ**		Econ Study	GYM	Shower & Dinner	Lounge & Relax	Stats & Calc Study	Stats & Calc Study
T	B&B	**Stats**	**Stats**	Stats & Calc Study	Stats & Calc Study	Lunch	**Calc**	**Calc**	**Calc (Recitation)**	GYM	Shower & Dinner	Lounge & Relax	Stats & Calc Study	Stats & Calc Study
W	B&B	IR Study	IR Study	IR Study	**Intl. Relations**	**Intl. Relations (Recitation)**	**Econ**	S N A C K	Econ Study	GYM	Shower & Dinner	Lounge & Relax	Stats & Calc Study	Stats & Calc Study
T	B&B	**Stats**	**Stats**	Stats & Calc Study	Stats & Calc Study	Lunch	**Calc**	**Calc**	Econ Study	GYM	Shower & Dinner	Lounge & Relax	Stats & Calc Study	Stats & Calc Study
F	B&B	Econ Study	Econ Study		**Intl. Relations**	Lunch	**Econ**		Econ Study	**Econ (Recitation)**	Dinner	Lounge & Relax		
S	S	L	E	E	P	E	A	T	&	P	A	R	T	Y
S	S	L	E	E	P	E	A	T	&	R	E	L	A	X

NOTE:

- This is a plan for free weekends with NO ORGANIZED activities like clubs or intramurals.
- There's decent school and fitness, but where's the other interesting stuff?
- Adding some activities during weekday evenings would require bumping some stuff to Sat/Sun.
- Opening up Sat/Sun would afford you another 24 hours for work & play (12 hours on both days).

191

WEEKLY PLANNER 2: Weeknight Activities

(CLASSES SHOWN IN BOLD: Statistics, International Relations, Economics, Calculus)

	8am	9	10	11	12	1pm	2	3	4	5	6	7	8	9
M	B&B *"Bathroom Routine & Breakfast*	IR Study	IR Study	IR Study	**Intl. Relations**	Lunch	**Econ**		Econ Study	GYM	Shower & Dinner	Lounge & Relax	Stats & Calc Study	Stats & Calc Study
T	B&B	**Stats**	**Stats**	Stats & Calc Study	Stats & Calc Study	Lunch	**Calc**	**Calc**	Econ Study	GYM	Shower & Dinner	Student Senate	Stats & Calc Study	Stats & Calc Study
W	B&B	IR Study	IR Study	IR Study	**Intl. Relations**	**Intl. Relations (Recita-tion)**	**Econ**	**Calc**	Econ Study	GYM	Dinner	Volley-ball	Stats & Calc Study	Stats & Calc Study
T	B&B	**Stats**	**Stats**	Stats & Calc Study	**Intl. Relations**	**Intl. Relations (Recita-tion)**	**Econ**	**Calc**	**Calc (Recita-tion)**	**Econ (Recita-tion)**	Dinner	Lounge & Relax	Stats & Calc Study	Stats & Calc Study
F	B&B	Econ Study	Econ Study	Stats & Calc Study	Stats & Calc Study	Lunch					Dinner	Lounge & Relax	Lounge & Relax	Lounge & Relax
S	S	L	E	E	P	E	A	T	&	P	A	R	T	Y
S	S	L	E	E	P	E	A	T	Stats & Calc Study				Lounge & Relax	Lounge & Relax

NOTE:

- Two (2) new weekday activities: Student Senate & Volleyball.
- Requires bumping Tues/Thurs evening studying to the weekend.
- Thursday night could now have some free time between 5-7pm (no GYM/Shower before volleyball?)
- Sunday was able to absorb 4 hours of Stats & Calc study and 2 hours of Lounging & Relaxing
- WHAT?! Saturday still had plenty of time for sleep, eat & party?! This is getting interesting....

WEEKLY PLANNER 3: Weekend Part-time Job

(CLASSES SHOWN IN BOLD: Statistics, International Relations, Economics, Calculus)

	8am	9	10	11	12	1pm	2	3	4	5	6	7	8	9
M	B&B* *Bathroom Routine & Breakfast	IR Study	IR Study	IR Study	**Intl. Relations**	Lunch	**Econ**	**Calc**	Econ Study	GYM	Shower & Dinner	Lounge & Relax	Stats & Calc Study	Stats & Calc Study
T	B&B	**Stats**	**Stats**	Stats & Calc Study	Stats & Calc Study	Lunch	**Calc**	**Calc**	**Calc (Recita-tion)**	GYM	Shower & Dinner	Student Senate	↑	
W	B&B	IR Study	IR Study	IR Study	**Intl. Relations**	**Intl. Relations (Recita-tion)**	**Econ**	**Calc**	Econ Study	GYM	Shower & Dinner	Lounge & Relax	Stats & Calc Study	Stats & Calc Study
T	B&B	**Stats**	**Stats**	Stats & Calc Study	Stats & Calc Study	Lunch	**Calc**	**Calc**	Econ Study	GYM	Shower & Dinner	Volley-ball	↑	
F	B&B	Econ Study	Econ Study		**Intl. Relations**	Lunch	**Econ**	**Calc**	Econ Study	**Econ (Recita-tion)**	Dinner	JOB		↑
S	SLEEP	↑	↑		EAT	J	O	B		→				
S	SLEEP	↑	↑		CHURCH	E	A	T	Stats & Calc Study		→	Lounge & Relax	Lounge & Relax	Lounge & Relax

NOTE:
- STILL have all your study time, fun activities, eating and relaxing accounted for.
- Fri & Sat now have hours for part-time job.
- Saturday's got work, but there's some sleepin' in, too.
- Sunday's even got time for church (so you can pray for good grades)!

WEEKLY PLANNER 4: The Big Game (aka Carpe F***ing College!)
(CLASSES SHOWN IN BOLD: Statistics, International Relations, Economics, Calculus)

	8am	9	10	11	12	1pm	2	3	4	5	6	7	8	9
M	B&B*	Stats	Stats	Stats & Calc Study	**Intl. Relations**	**Intl. Relations (Recita-tion)**	**Econ**		Econ Study	GYM	Shower & Dinner	Student Senate	Stats & Calc Study	Stats & Calc Study
T	B&B	IR Study	IR Study	IR Study	Stats & Calc Study	Lunch	**Calc**	**Calc**	Econ Study	GYM	Shower & Dinner	Lounge & Relax	Stats & Calc Study	Stats & Calc Study
W	B&B	Stats	Stats	Stats & Calc Study	**Intl. Relations (Recita-tion)**	**Intl. Relations (Recita-tion)**	**Econ**		Econ Study	GYM	Dinner	Volley-ball	Stats & Calc Study	Stats & Calc Study
T	B&B	IR Study	IR Study	IR Study	Lunch	Lunch	**Calc**	**Calc**	**Calc (Recita-tion)**	**Econ (Recita-tion)**	Dinner	Lounge & Relax	Stats & Calc Study	Stats & Calc Study
F	B&B	**Stats**	**Stats**	Stats & Calc Study	**Intl. Relations**	Lunch	**Econ**		Econ Study	Econ Study	Dinner	JOB		
S	SLEEP (→)				THE	BIG	G	A	M	E				
S	SLEEP (→)				CHURCH	J	O	B						

*"Bathroom Routine & Breakfast"

NOTE:
- The BIG GAME throws off the plans a bit, displacing some Stats & Calc study.
- Extend your weeknight study times till 11pm, and you'll be okay, even with ALL this stuff.
- This plan gives you appropriate studies plus fun, fitness, faith, and furthering your leadership skills!
- Play around with these 'puzzle pieces' & rearrange them as you see fit to make it work for you.

WEEKLY PLANNER 5: Winging It! (aka A Recipe for Trouble)
(CLASSES SHOWN IN BOLD: Statistics, International Relations, Economics, Calculus)

	8am	9	10	11	12	1pm	2	3	4	5	6	7	8	9
M	B&B* *Bathroom Routine & Breakfast*	Sleep	Sleep	Sleep	**Intl. Relations**	Lunch	**Econ**		Econ Study	GYM	Shower & Dinner	Lounge & Relax	Study Whatever	Study Whatever
T	B&B	**Stats**	**Stats**	Nap	Nap	Lunch	**Calc**	**Calc**	**Calc (Recita-tion)**	GYM	Shower & Dinner	Lounge & Relax	Study Whatever	Study Whatever
W	B&B	Sleep	Sleep	Sleep	**Intl. Relations**	**Intl. Relations (Recita-tion)**	**Econ**	L U N C H	Nap	GYM	Shower & Dinner	Lounge & Relax	Study Whatever	Study Whatever
T	B&B	**Stats**	**Stats**	Nap	Nap	Lunch	**Calc**	**Calc**	Dorm Hang Out	GYM	Shower & Dinner	Lounge & Relax	Study Whatever	Study Whatever
F	B&B	Sleep	Sleep	Sleep	**Intl. Relations**	Lunch	**Econ**	Nap	Dorm Hang Out	**Econ (Recita-tion)**	Dinner	Lounge & Relax		
S	S	L	E	E	P	E	A	T	&	P	A	R	T	Y
S	S	L	E	E	P	E	A	T	&	R	E	L	A	X

NOTE: This 'plan' isn't really a plan. While it has the appearance of a plan, there's no real structure except for the course schedule. This student might make it to class, get some rest, stay fit, socialize, and get some studying in. HOWEVER, without more detailed planning, the demands of schoolwork will take over within a few weeks, nudging the other stuff out of the way. Or, the schoolwork will simply take a back seat to everything else. Compare this 'plan' to The Big Game plan to see what a big difference a little planning can do.

APPENDIX D:
CHECKING-IN CHART (ACADEMICS)

Here's a handy chart with questions designed to get you reflecting on how your first term went academically, how you feel about it, and thoughts about whether you may have to make some mid-year modifications. If this format doesn't work for you, take out a journal or your laptop and just start writing about your first year. It'll all come out that way, too.

REFLECTIVE QUESTIONS	ANSWERS, NOTES & RESOURCES
How did first term go (generally speaking)? Are you feeling good about it, or not so good?	
What do you want to be able to say in June? Do you have a GPA number/goal in your head?	
Based on where you are right now and where you'd like to be in June, how's your progress?	
On a scale of 1 (terrible) to 10 (wonderful), rate your overall academic experience so far?	
Is there anything YOUR SCHOOL or YOU could do differently to improve that evaluation?	
What have been your greatest academic successes and challenges? How did you address the challenges? How did you savor the success?	
What does SUNDAY NIGHT look like? Stressed?	
If you would like it to be different, how can you adjust your planning?	
How do you keep track of your life? How detailed is your planning? How has that worked?	
Do you study in your dorm room? How has that worked? Any better locations?	
Do you know exactly where you stand in all your classes week to week? How do you keep track? How do you reach out to your professor if you don't have the information you need?	

Given your responses to all of the above, what are the most important adjustments you need to make for next term?

APPENDIX D:
CHECKING-IN CHART (NON-ACADEMICS)

Just like your academic check-in, this chart should help you reflect on how things went outside the classroom. Again, if you don't like charts, just start writing, or have a friend read these questions to you and record it. (Then you can do a mash-up, combining it with your favorite Justin Bieber song.)

REFLECTIVE QUESTIONS	ANSWERS, NOTES & RESOURCES
How did first term go (generally speaking)? Are you feeling good about it, or not so good?	
What do you want to be able to say in June about your social life?	
How's your progress?	
On a scale of 1 (terrible) to 10 (wonderful), rate your overall non-academic experience so far?	
Is there anything YOUR SCHOOL or YOU could do differently to improve that evaluation?	
Is dorm life good? (Roommate, dorm mates, social, dinner, etc.)	
Any social miscues? Were you able to Fix It? Forgive? Forge Ahead?	
What have been your greatest NON-academic successes and challenges?	
Are you eating well, exercising & sleeping well?	
Are you playing Bulletin Board Bingo each month?	
Are you playing "Poppin' in to see the Prof" at the beginning of each term? (Long-term relationships!)	
Have you reached out to professionals for shadowing experiences or potential internships?	

Given your responses to all of the above, what are the most important adjustments you need to make for next term?

APPENDIX E:
HOMESTRETCH E-MAIL (TO ALL YOUR PROFS)

As you head into the homestretch before final exams (or mid-terms for that matter), it's important to know EXACTLY where you stand in ALL of your classes. I often poll my students during this homestretch, and I'm amazed at how many of them are unsure of their current grades. They're not keeping tabs, and they're not checking in with professors. (Or their profs are slow to update the grades, and the students are waiting passively by.)

Don't assume you 'think' you know where you stand. Your perception (and math) may be quite different from your professors and, even though grading policies are all laid out on the syllabus, it's always good to double check. I've heard of cases where professors decided to drop the lowest test score or exempt students from their final exam if they were carrying an 'A' average. I also heard of a student who THOUGHT she was doing poorly in a class, but the professor's grading scale had her at a 'B' grade within striking distance of an 'A'. She dropped the class before checking in with the professor!

There is a better way.

Fire off a simple email to each professor to ensure you're both on the same page. Here's a sample, and you can fill in your own content based on each course:

> Dear [Professor Plum]:
>
> I'm getting ready for the homestretch before finals, and I was hoping to run my game plan by you.
>
> My records indicate that I have a --% grade in our class currently, and my hope is to do the following between now and finals:
>
> 1. Review [A, B,and C] with particular attention to [blah, blah and blah].
>
> 2. Finish strong with the [FILL IN THE BLANK] project.
>
> 3. Work with my study partners on [LIST IMPORTANT CONCEPTS].
>
> 4. Attend all the review sessions.
>
> Do you think this is a good plan? Do you have any further advice? Would it be okay if I came in to chat about this?
>
> Thanks so much.
>
> [YOUR NAME HERE}
> [YOUR CLASS TIME/DATE/SECTION # HERE]

NOTE: If your professor is sitting on a stack of papers or tests, trying to wade her way through it, and if your paper is near the bottom of that stack, you could wait and wait and wait. But if you're the one who sends the email or stops in to her office to see where you stand, she just might move yours to the top of the stack and give you the quick answer you've been hoping for. Why not act?!

APPENDIX E:
HOMESTRETCH ADVICE

Beginning with that all-important 'check-in' with professors, here's my list of advice to help you prepare for that first (or second, or third, or ninth) round of final exams.

THE ADVICE	THE DETAILS
Know where you stand in every class.	Send those emails to your profs (or stop in).
Be an advocate for yourself by utilizing resources.	Seek help from peers, study partners, TA's, review sessions, professors. Attend review sessions, math labs, and the campus writing center. At the very least, have 'another set of eyes' look at EVERY paper before you turn it in.
Double check syllabus for deadlines & requirements.	It's the CONTRACT! Don't overlook something.
Designate review time EACH DAY in homestretch.	• Break material into workable chunks (1 hr/class) • Take frequent stretch breaks (for blood flow, socializing, texting – but stay on schedule) • Study sessions must be DISTRACTION-FREE (Quiet space & shut off that phone!)
Remember brain research says to PLAY with info.	• Study groups, flash cards, re-writing notes, visual maps, conversing = PLAYING with info • Remember 'See one. Do one. Teach one.' • Plan for RECALL rather than RECOGNITION test
Take care of mind & body.	• Good planning means better sleep schedule • Read a fun book (1 chapter) before lights out • Avoid screens (TV/laptop) 1-hour before sleeping
Plan for 'The June Question' You will be asked in June, "How was your first year?" Think about what you'd like your response to be, and then think about how you can get there. This also works on a short-term basis. What do I want to be able to say at the end of THIS week? At the end of THIS semester? How can I get there?	• You answer ONLY TO YOURSELF • Follow process: setting goals & planning strategy • Execute by managing your time, building a plan, and sticking to it • You have done this kind of planning, juggling and managing throughout high school, and you've done it successfully. But now it's at an elevated level. So, you're completely capable of doing it if you take the time to think it through & stay disciplined.

APPENDIX F:
BOLSTERING YOUR BREAK:
THINKING BIG

You DEFINITELY want to recharge your battery over school breaks. However, it's also a great time to do some of that big thinking you may not have had time for while studying & socializing.

So, get your rest, have some fun, and relax. But once you're done with that, grab a good book to read, catch up on world news, and THINK BIG.

What's up with my career exploration? Job shadowing? Internship?
What's up with my passions *(Music, sports, history, entrepreneurial projects, etc.)?*
What 'Carpe College' experiences enriched me? What did I learn? *(Any good stuff for my resume?)*

APPENDIX G:
A NOTE TO STRUGGLING STUDENTS WHOSE FIRST YEAR GOES POORLY (WHICH SHOULDN'T HAVE HAPPENED IF YOU'D READ THIS DAMN BOOK! JK)

Dear Struggling Student:

It's important to remember that the first year is a very challenging transition. (Some suggest the degree of difficulty/trauma lies somewhere between being born and heading off to kindergarten – in other words, a pretty significant and challenging step in a person's life.) It's also important to remember that, while the college years will fly by, they should still be approached as a marathon rather than a sprint. And it's important to remember that you're just barely out of the gate.

At the end of all of this, you'll have a story to tell. It's like answering 'The June Question,' but it'll be three more Junes from now. That future June story will be more important than your current June story. If you had a great first year and plummeted for the next three, that would be a rough story to tell. But if you struggle your first year, right the ship, and finish your college career strong, that's an easy story to tell, and one that's been told time and time again.

Plenty of people struggle their first year, so that won't surprise any recruiter or grad school. But it's what you do from here on out that matters.

So, it's time once again to follow our mantra: *Know Thyself. Have a Plan. Assume No One Else Cares.*

Take a look at yourself and reassess your strengths, weaknesses and performance. Be honest! Take a look at your planning and how you executed that plan. Make changes! Take a moment to realize that it's you who must own this journey. Embrace it!

In addition to using your summer for such reevaluation and planning, maybe you can use your summer to retake a class that you didn't do that well in. Or take a class to get ahead, so you could take a lighter course load next year. Maybe you can re-tool and shore up some skills (Math? Writing? Study skills?) that need improving. Maybe you can make a list of all the campus resources that you can access EARLY next term to help you succeed.

No matter what, don't be discouraged. If you are honest with yourself, if you are open-minded about the improvements needed, if you realize that there are others who can help you, and if you put in the hard work to set things right, you WILL succeed, and you will have a great story to tell three Junes from now.

Stop looking to your left and to your right and making comparisons to others. Simply take your reins and giddyup!

Yours truly.

APPENDIX H:
COMMUTER (AND COMMUNITY COLLEGE) CARE PACKAGE

"...the road is life."
— JACK KEROUAC

The commuter student's life is... well... different. It's not the same as other students because of one important variable: geography. Location. Location. Location. It's all about getting from Point A to Point B and giving up Point C. You're living at home, driving (or riding) to school and back, and missing out on dorm living. In addition to location, there is also the matter of time. You will be traveling, which takes time, and you may have limited time with your fellow students compared to dorm dwellers. This existence does not have to be viewed in terms of positives and negatives, however. It just is. You may have chosen it. It may have been foisted upon you. There were probably choices made by you and your family all along the way. Regardless, recognizing what this student lifestyle offers or doesn't offer is important to making the most of it.

Here's a list of some POSSIBLE haves and have-nots for commuter students:

Haves	Have-nots
Freedom to leave campus	Dorm living (place to crash)
Transportation costs	Easy peer relationships
Travel stress	Time (lost during commute)
Outside responsibilities	Connectedness
Part-time job	Spontaneous social life
Money saved	
Living space	

Now, this list isn't going to apply to every commuter in every case, and it's not an exhaustive one. Maybe you're not living at home with your family, or maybe they're paying for transportation costs, or maybe your cell phone is all you need to feel 'connected'. The point is that your commuter lifestyle will be different from most students, primarily in terms of relationships and time. Here are some thoughts....

RELATIONSHIPS

A lot of social stuff revolves around the residence halls. Dorm mates go to dinner together, goof around, plan their weekends, and hang out, which provides a certain spontaneity that's hard to come by if you're not living there. Relationships are forged early and on a daily basis in dorm living, and it's nearly impossible for a commuter student to be an integral part of that. But that doesn't mean you need to 'miss out.' You might just need a different plan for a different lifestyle.

From a social standpoint, commuters can't just wing-it like their dorm dwelling counterparts. You'll need a plan to meet new people. You'll need to know what your social goals are and what kind of social time you'll have week to week. Be creative and consider lots of options. Since you won't be in the dorms to forge daily social bonds, you'll have to work harder at it. You could stay over night in a friend's dorm room at least once per month, or eat dinner on campus on a regular basis. Since you won't have dorm mates, you could work harder at getting to know classmates by inviting them to join you for lunch. You could invite fellow students home to your house to give them a break from campus, or offer to be their driver to go to the local mall. You could get involved in a campus organization or activity that 'forces' you to stay on campus in the evenings and be with peers on a regular basis.

Again, consider your personal goals and have a plan. Because your existence is different from dorm dwellers, you will need to be active and intentional about forging social relationships.

REAL ESTATE

As mentioned earlier, you're going to be shuttling between Point A and Point B for most of your college commuter existence. It doesn't really matter if A is home and B is campus, or vice versa. What matters is that you'll have to manage time and space as it relates to these two places.

Let's say that you decide to make a real earnest effort to meet new people, you try some of the 'strategies' listed above, you establish some decent friendships, and you're staying overnight crashing in friends' rooms on a regular basis. It may be tough to determine what 'home' is. But who cares? If you're ever going to be a nomad, your college years are the right time for it. Any time spent on campus should help you build stronger connections to the campus community, so seize and relish those opportunities. Why not have an overnight bag pre-packed and tossed in your car, along with a sleeping bag, so you can be as spontaneous as those dorm-dwellers?!

More important than your social life, however, is your school life. How you manage your campus space and time will affect how you perform. You don't have the luxury of a dorm room to unwind in, so you'll need to utilize as much of the campus space and resources as possible. After the first few weeks, you should have a pretty good sense of the coffee shops and lounges throughout campus, as well as the library layout. Eventually, you'll be able to identify good places for socializing and people watching, good places for quiet studying, and good places for a quick nap. Most campuses will even have an office dedicated to commuter students, offering study and social space and other resources. Once you get a handle on where all this stuff is, you can manage your on-campus time.

(If you're fortunate, you'll also have a dedicated study space at home, free of distractions and obligations. If you can't secure this, then use campus as your refuge.)

Imagine heading to your favorite quiet lounge spot between morning classes to get some studying done. Then you meet friends from class for lunch at a more social and raucous eatery in the middle of the day. You head back to your quiet space between afternoon classes, then head to the dorm cafeteria or food court to meet other friends for dinner. One of your study groups meets in the library after dinner, which caps off your evening. If you've got an evening activity, like intramurals or a campus organization meeting, just plug that in. By the end of the evening, you will have covered a lot of ground on campus, getting work accomplished and enjoying time with friends. That's a great use of time and campus space from a commuter's standpoint, and if you conduct yourself in this manner, your experience won't be that far removed from the dorm dwellers.

RESPONSIBILITIES

Being a college student is inherently egocentric and selfish because you're focused on you, your development, and your future. Your focus is very much inward, centering on your goals, your space and your schedule. One advantage for commuters is that they typically have obligations to family or work outside of their school responsibilities, and this can be quite beneficial for long-term development (and for resumes).

So, everything that's been mentioned above has to be tailored to your own specific lifestyle and collection of responsibilities. If you need to be home in the evenings to babysit a younger sibling, or if your part-time job books you for most of the weekend, then that will dictate how you manage your social life. Presumably, school will be your number one priority, and the others will fall in line. Typically, a social life can get pushed to the back burner, but with some finesse, you can have that, too.

HERE ARE SOME RANDOM TIPS TO CARPE THAT COMMUTER LIFESTYLE:

- Plan to stay late and attend ALL of the orientation activities offered in the fall. If any of the socializing spills over to the dorms later at night, go with the crowd. The beginning days are critical for establishing relationships, and if you can tap into the dorm part of that early on, it could pay off later.
  (Discuss this approach with your parents or employer ahead of time, emphasizing the importance of the first weeks of school. If you can get a break from home or work responsibilities early on, you can establish some social ties on campus and pick up the slack elsewhere later on.)
- Be as outgoing as possible in your classes and work hard to establish study partners and groups. For some commuters, the classroom could be your PRIMARY source of social connections. Going to lunch with classmates or exchanging phone numbers to set up study sessions are great ways to warm up those social connections.
- If you have a part-time job, leverage your status as a responsible college kid. Presumably, you're more mature than a high schooler, and you're more serious about your goals. This should make you a more attractive employee and, because of that, your employer might be willing to accommodate scheduling around your school and social needs. It absolutely cannot hurt to ask!
- Is your place of employment a place that would want college kids at their establishment? If so, why not ask your employer to give you an extra hour break if you bring in a group of your college friends. So, if you're working on a Saturday night at a restaurant, maybe you could invite your friends to stop in for dinner before they go out partying, and maybe your manager will let you take an extended break and sit with them for an hour during your work shift. Your boss wins by gaining new business. You win by getting an extra chance to socialize with your friends while putting in your time at work.
  (I told you this might take some creativity!)
- Use your travel time wisely. Listen to the news. Turn off the radio and record your ideas (alone time in the car is just like the shower or the toilet – the ideas just seem to flow when you have no place you can go). Or, try practicing a skill, like my son's friend Demetrio did. He's a

great drummer, and he wanted to continue to improve, so he took one drumstick, put it in his weaker hand, and worked on his stick control, speed and stamina during his drives to and from campus. Fortunately, he did not get charged with a DWD – Driving While Drumming. (I know that joke sucked, but I left it in anyway. Deal with it.)

> *If you want to see Demitrio's great drumming, check him out as "Drumzoo" on YouTube.*

- Manage your time and space. As mentioned previously, plan with your priorities in mind (school, work, family, social, etc.) and plan to use your entire day and your entire campus. If you can find the right time and place for studying and socializing on campus, and if you work wisely to stay connected, you can find a balance that works for you.

Maybe you can have it all!!

APPENDIX I:
STUDENT ATHLETES: SEPARATE BUT EQUAL?

'Life must be lived as play.''
— PLATO

Maybe by this point you're tired of people telling you how special you are. Or maybe you're still basking in it. Either way, that's going to be a part of your student-athlete life for the next few years, and there's no getting around it. You are special, you will be treated as though you're special, and yet your goals are probably the same as every other 'regular' student (unless you plan to be a professional athlete or Olympian). You want to graduate with knowhow and skills to begin a career and become a thoughtful, well-functioning citizen.

But you're not like 'normal' students because you have expectations, obligations, and special treatment that they don't have. You have team meetings, training, practices, meals, travel, games, community-relations events, and aches and pains that can't help but dig into your academic time. Everyone associated with NCAA athletics will tell you that there's a good reason you're called a 'student-athlete' with the student part first and academics as the priority. When you're immersed in a weekly regimen of 'team time,' however, it may be hard to focus on your life outside your sport. And when you're showered with special stuff (special course registration, special meals, special gear, special travel, special opportunities in the community, special status, etc.), it might become hard to stay grounded and maintain perspective.

So, it might be beneficial to remember our mantra

Know Thyself. Have a Plan. Assume No One Else Cares.

KNOW THYSELF

In high school athletics, you were a 'big fish.' It may take you a while to get back to that stature at the college level. Or, you may never get back there. Is school your Plan B? I would recommend making it your Plan A. This does not mean to abandon your athletic dreams. Keep them alive, continue to perfect your skills and perform at your best level, and *enjoy* this wonderful experience that only a small number of college students get to enjoy. But before school begins in the fall, please spend some serious time thinking about your life after athletics. Put all your athletic plans aside *temporarily* and consider who you are and who you wish to become *without* athletics.

Remember that you are the one who's still in control of your own destiny. At least in terms of planning for your present and future. You made an agreement with your institution that you would partake in their athletics program, but their part of the bargain was that they would educate you. What kind of education do you want? What do you want to do with it when you're done? Go back and review some of the advice contained in this book and see if you can find a way to find your bliss apart from your sport. This should help drive how you approach the academic side of your life for the next few years.

It's also important to remember there will be multiple sides to your life over your college career. You might play the role of a campus leader and an ambassador for your team and your school. It's healthy to consider how others might view you and how you'd like to view yourself in this capacity. You could start by reflecting on how you acted back in high school when you were a celebrated student-athlete. Were you a good student, teammate and person? Were you a good role model? In other words, did you find a way to transcend being identified only by the sport you played? Were you able to be something else first?

I sat next to a Heisman Trophy runner-up in one of my marketing classes. He and I exchanged small talk and class notes and, later in life, when he became a college football coach, he sent my son some fun autographed memorabilia to inspire him as he began his young football 'career.' This guy was a true Big Man On Campus, but he allowed me to see him as simply a nice, humble guy by the way he carried himself.

One of my son's friends, Conner, who's going on to play Division I baseball, proposes this outlook for a student-athlete to maintain proper stature and perspective: "Stay focused. Stay smart. Stay humble." These are wise words, and you've probably heard something like it from your coaches, parents or recruiters along the way. But it's time that you begin to interpret them in terms of your own outlook and your own behavior.

HAVE A PLAN

Let's keep this simple… and harsh. Tomorrow you blow out your knee and end your athletic career. What's your plan?

Sorry to be so blunt, but this is the best way to figure out if you have truly thought through your plans. I'd recommend reflection on what your goals are, who you want to be, as a person, as a student, and as an athlete. Treat them all separately at first, and then combine them into one larger plan. Of course, what you do over the next few years as a student and an athlete will help forge who you can become as a person, but it's always good to start with the bigger 'person' picture, knowing that your days as a student and as an athlete will eventually fade away. So, begin with 'Who do I wish to become and how do I want people to see me?' and work your way back from there.

Once you're done planning who you wish to be as a person, you can use what you've read in this book to plan what you'd like your student life to look like. Then, once you're done with that, move on to your athletic life. Revisit 'The June Question' to think about what you'd like to say after your first athletic year. Or aim higher and consider what you'd like to be able to say when your college athletic career is done. Once you've reflected on these matters on your own, be sure to share them with your coach, parents and others who care about you.

After laying out all this planning, it's important to return to the fact that your life as a student-athlete makes for a somewhat different college experience than most students. It will require one more bit of planning: your social life. The easy way to do it would be to meet your teammates and do whatever the team does. If that's the extent of what you're looking for from your college experience, then stick with it. But because of your situation, you have the unique opportunity to carpe more college than most. Consider how you're going to meet your dorm mates. Of course, you'll spend a ton of time with your teammates, but what if you planned one day a week to stroll your dorm halls and say hello to people who aren't on the team? What about *Bulletin Board Bingo?* With your busy team schedule, it's going to be tough to find time to experience all the great cultural offerings on campus. But if you have a plan, you can do it. Are things a little lighter for you off-season? Why not plan to do some *Bulletin Board Bingo* then? You might even be able to combine that with meeting dorm mates. To the best of your ability, and in terms of what your schedule will allow, try to reach out and away from your athletic culture as early and as often as you can. That will make for a richer overall college experience, and you'll be able to say, in a way few others can, that you really carpe'd college.

Note: For planning purposes, try to utilize the entire year to fit in all that you'd like to accomplish. Consider that you'll be swamped while your sport is in season, but when out of season, with fewer travel concerns, you may find time to squeeze in some of this other stuff. Week to week, you're simply not going to be able to fit it all in, and you won't have nearly the time luxuries that other students have. However, over the course of a full year, you will. Again, it's all about what you'd like to be able to say at the end of the year.

ASSUME NO ONE ELSE CARES

Simply apply this part of the mantra to your athletic life the same way you're doing for your student life. It's your job to run your life, and you need to care about it more than anyone else. Of course you should rely on coaches, professors, parents, teammates and tutors, but you've got to rely on yourself more.

As mentioned earlier in this book, it's not that your teammates or fellow students aren't nice people. It's just that they have themselves to worry about. If you decide to break team rules and get suspended for a few weeks, I'm sure a teammate will gladly step in and take your starting position for game day. If you forget to tell your professor about your team travel plans, it's unlikely anyone else will. Even if your team offers some formal communication with professors, having a special travel schedule gives you a built-in excuse to talk to your professors and get to know them better. And we've already addressed why that's a good thing.

Again, I'm sorry, but what if you blow out your knee and end your career? Is there anyone who will care more about your next move than you? A friend of mine earned an athletic scholarship to a Big Ten football program with a stellar academic reputation. He blew out his knee before his first season without playing a down for the team, and his career ended. The school, however, honored his scholarship until graduation. So, you see, assuming no one cares is not meant to make you cynical and jaded; it's designed to help you plan for the worst while hoping for the best. It's about having YOU in control of your journey even though there are a whole lot of uncontrollable factors that can come into play. If you have planned in this way, good things can fall into place even after some setbacks.

What if you want to be something more than just an athlete? What if you want to have friends outside your team? What if you want to go on to grad school? What if you want to do philanthropic work in the local community or abroad? What if you want to be a head coach some day? What if you can't afford to be charged with a crime because your future is riding on your college experience? What if you want to be nice to everyone?

All of these answers must reside with you. You can lay the groundwork with some deep self-reflection and a good plan that begins your first year.

You'll have a unique opportunity to have a much more rich college experience than most.

Seize it!

APPENDIX J:
FREE ADVICE FROM FORMER FIRST-YEARS

When I started teaching first-year college students, I reached out to all of my former high school students who had gone off to college and asked them to offer advice to incoming college students. I've made this request of all of my students every year since then, and the collection of their advice is what follows.

Yes, it's long and extensive and unedited, for the most part, because it's in their own words. Feel free to just scan through it and find some wisdom that speaks to you. I've collected the advice into general categories and then thrown a bunch of their miscellaneous insights & notes into a hodgepodge at the end. I caught some of these students at the end of their first year, some in their later college years, and some after they had graduated, so you'll see those perspectives reflected in their comments

Know that it came from REAL college students who REALLY wanted to pay it forward and help you out. So, the advice is way better than anything I could have ever told you!

Enjoy!

THE MOST DIFFICULT PART OF MY FIRST YEAR WAS...

Meeting new people.

Time management.

The first semester. You are stuck in an awkward stage of not knowing many people on campus and trying to maintain the relationships from home. You are in the process of getting involved with clubs and activities and working to break into these social circles at college. This isn't always easy and sometimes doesn't work out which can lead to a feeling of being alone without any help on campus or anyone to turn to right near by. Once you get past that first semester, however, you start building relationships with people of similar interests and are to the point where you are beginning to see the same faces in various classes and form friendships with these people and you begin to settle into a group on campus. This point is when college begins to feel like home and it becomes far less scary and much more rewarding and fun.

Feeling like an outsider--not really knowing what to do, where to go, what I was doing, and constantly having to ask people how to get very simple things done. Not really "getting" the campus culture, and not being sure if I belonged there. Missing my family.

I had an awkward roommate situation. Dealing with the tension in my own room was probably the most challenging because it was so unexpected.

... being away from home. I attended a large university where one can feel like a "number" in the crowd. And... family has always been important to me and I was fortunate to grow up in a very loving and supportive family. So, to be away from that for the first time in a fairly impersonal environment was difficult. And I think not finding a lot of people that I "connected with" made being away from home a little more difficult. Looking back, I know my involvement in organizations within the school helped me start to feel "at home" because it made the school feel smaller.

This sounds silly, but it really was the hardest part... it was realizing that the first boy I dated was NOT going to be my future husband. It was fun to date him, but it was hard to realize that I had four years at this amazing school and in those four years I was going to change, and so was that guy. It was also hard for me to think that there may be an even better guy out there for me (which I did meet my junior year and am still with).

Adjusting to weekend dorm life and an erratic new sleeping schedule.

Getting my head around the options and myriad ways to "make the most" of college and the larger city I'd inhabit but never really live in.

Honestly, the hardest part for me was finding a good eating schedule. I like building my schedule so that I have all of my classes earlier and back-to-back. Often, that would mean no sufficient break to get food. I would typically wake up too late for breakfast and would end up eating lunch around 2. I was always starving! Try to work a time to eat into your schedule and stick to that time if you can!

Coming to terms with the fact that I wasn't as well prepared academically as I should have been. This was really tough for me to accept, and it caused a lot of stress early on in the year.

THE MOST WONDERFUL PART OF MY FIRST YEAR WAS...

Great time, living on your own, doing what you want, making your own schedule, freedom is nice.

The feeling of accomplishment at the end of it. It's not that I was saying "Oh I can't wait to get out of here!" but more of a feeling of pride in that despite the struggles every freshman faces I was able to persevere.

The freedom.

Self-determination. Most of the time, my parents had no idea what I was up to unless I told them--that I could study basically anything I wanted, stay up as late as I wanted, play MarioKart instead of doing homework, and order pizza at 2am. I could date someone and not tell them about it. Some of that was really scary, being responsible for myself and not really having someone there to remind me that a lot of that might have been kind of dumb, but I came out on the other side much more confident in my ability to be a big kid one day.

There are too many to name! I think my alternative spring break experience will probably make the short list of my college career.

...finishing! I remember feeling very proud to complete my first year in college because it was not easy and it was my first test of my ability to take care of myself.

Everything! If I had to go back and do a year of college over again it would be my first year. It was great.

Meeting new friends with diverse backgrounds.

THE ONE THING I'D BE SURE TO DO IF I WERE A FIRST-YEAR AGAIN...

Meet everyone on my floor.

Listen to those trying to help you out in the beginning. Many schools have a network of help available to you and student peer advisors and contacts that will try to help throughout the beginning of school (even an RA is an excellent resource because of their large amounts of training and knowledge). In all of my infinite wisdom I didn't need them at the time, however it didn't take long before I started having questions and friends and floor mates began having the answers and when asked how they knew they would respond with "Well, I asked my peer advisor and they helped me find the answer." Utilize the support services that the college has in place because that's why they are there. I didn't use them because I didn't think I had to but I quickly learned that many things would have been easier for me if I asked for help from those around me who were there to help.

Make friends with upperclassmen. My older and wiser comrades not only helped me figure out what my school was about, but were also great mentors and teachers. Also, it turns out, upperclassmen love collecting pet freshmen. It makes us feel useful.

.... take a variety of classes (especially if you are unsure about what you want to do with your life, from a career standpoint, as I was). Don't rush through school thinking that you HAVE to finish in 4 years. I would rather take 4.5-5 years with a degree I am passionate about instead of rushing through and not really being excited about your career prospects. College is a great time to discover what you are really interested in because you have so much information at your fingertips!

Get to know upperclassmen as well as people from my class. They showed me some things about the college that I would have never figured out if it wasn't for them. I would also not lean on my friends from my hometown as much as I did in the beginning.

Treat used textbook buying like a science.

Don't panic when faced with stressful new challenges. There are so many people available to help you here, and they all want you to be successful, including your professors (even if you are struggling in their classes). Don't panic and definitely don't give up. Hard work will get you through it.

The one thing I'd be sure to do if I were a freshman again is to just get involved! I have made so many new, awesome friends by joining so many different organizations around campus! When you get involved in different organizations that interest you, you meet other people that have those same interests and those friends end up becoming friends for life. Also, you never know how much joining just one organization can truly change your life.

THE ONE THING I'D BE SURE NEVER TO DO AGAIN....

Not study before a test or go out the night before a test.

Say "No Thanks" to the late night movie sessions in the floor common room or on going to play basketball and social things of the like. As a relatively shy person freshman year for me meant a lot of staying in my room talking to friends from home and not trying to build friendships at school. This was a big mistake and something I would definitely do differently if I had the chance. Friends from home will always be there when you go back. By missing out on doing a lot of social things around campus I missed out on a lot of friendships with people that I probably would have gotten along with very well. If I could do it over I would try to find a better balance of socializing with old friends from home and new friends at school.

Be dead set on a course of study. The major I thought I would love turned out to feel boring and limiting by the end of my sophomore year. Luckily, I was mostly done with it, but I wish I had found out that another subject was really endlessly fascinating.

Take certain classes just because my friends were. I probably would have saved a lot of time and money on classes I didn't need if I hadn't done that. I also probably would have met more people.

The one thing I'd be sure to never do again is forget why we're all truly here... to get a degree. There will be so many cool events, and opportunities that will come your way but you can't forget to always put academics first! You can't forget that academics is the real reason why we are all truly here.

THE SMARTEST THING I DID IN MY FIRST YEAR...
DON'T PROCRASTINATE!

Start becoming more organized. In high school I was never the type to write down meetings and big assignments or tests. In college it seems that everything happens at once and if you don't plan it out and keep track of your appointments, assignments, and exams it will be very easy to let one slip without taking care of it. It seems that as my educational process continues the importance of being organized becomes more and more apparent. There will be weeks when you may have several exams and budgeting the time out to ensure that each gets its' deserved amount of studying is the only way to do it.

Study... a lot.

Make time to spend with friends. Even though I was panicking most of the time about not stacking up academically, it was definitely worth it to institute a no-homework-on-Fridays rule. (Also makes you feel a little better about being in the library until it closes on Friday nights all through junior year because, Hey, wistfully, you had your fun.)

Network with professors and students especially the ones outside of my major.

Not to get caught up in my grades and studying. I made sure that I studied and did my homework, but I also made sure that I had time to relax and hang out with my friends. I didn't want to be the person who looked back on their college career and regret worrying so much about my grades and not enjoying myself. Like my Dad said right before he left after dropping me off, "Work hard, play hard."

Take a dance class.

I'm a crazy scheduler and have pretty good time management. I did homework the day it was assigned and did papers and projects right away. Don't EVER save them for the last minute. Your grade will reflect it. Learn time management and a system that works for you to keep your due dates straight for each class. I use a big desk calendar that I can write all over and see what I have coming up over the course of the week – but more importantly the long term projects I have that are often easily forgotten!

Well I'm just finishing my first year now, but my smartest academic move so far has just been honest hard work. Work hard at your goals and you will succeed. My transition from high school academics to college academics was anything but smooth, however I adapted quickly and have had a very successful academic year.

Never intentionally skipping class. If you break down tuition for the year per class session, you waste a lot of money by not showing up.

Realized it's not about being the brightest or most innovative, but rather being the one who can best work the system.

The smartest thing I did as a freshman was not letting just one thing define me. Many people will just try one thing on campus or just do one thing on campus and just decide that they want it to define them. I have seen and met people that the only thing they ever want to talk about is that one club or team that they're on and it's like, I am happy you are happy in that organization and even if I'd like to learn more about it, It's not the only thing I want to talk about either.

I reevaluated my priorities, work ethic, and being as a whole and turned my grades around tenfold.

Keep all my notes from previous classes to help with a class the following quarter. Unlike high school, a lot of what you learn will actually help later.

THE DUMBEST THING I DID IN MY FIRST YEAR...

Not ask for help when I needed. It led to feelings of being overwhelmed and hopelessness at times, which would have been totally avoidable if I had asked the simple questions as they came up rather than letting them snowball together until there were too many questions to know where to start.

Do you really want to know?! lol

Feel intimidated by my professors and older classmates. Especially professors. It turns out they do want to talk to you and have you at their office hours.

...attempting to get a guy to like me. He really wasn't my type, it didn't go anywhere (except for a little embarrassment on my part), and therefore, he wasn't worth the effort. Dating can be a very big part of people's college experience. If that is an important part of life, just remember that when you find the right person... it happens naturally! You won't have to "work" at it.

I got really drunk one night and was walking down a big hill and fell... which led to me calling my parents in the middle of the night and explaining to them that I had just broken my ankle and they needed to come get me. We laugh about it now, but it was not funny at the time!

I threw my ID away at lunch one day and didn't realize it until I tried to get back in my dorm. Never leave your ID on your tray!

Get drunk the night before a track meet.

Treat my studies cavalierly and indifferently continue (successfully) the B average attitude that let me coast through High School.

Decide to attempt to de-loft my bed alone… Definitely get at least one other person to help or your bed will come tumbling down all around you.

Not eating before I went to go workout once. I passed out for two seconds, but had to visit the hospital for 4 hours, then pay a cab $17 to drive me five minutes back to campus.

Stored my roommate's beer in my refrigerator.

The dumbest thing I did as a freshman was procrastinating on some assignments. In high school, if you procrastinate, you'll end up spending a couple hours to fix that assignment. In college, if you procrastinate on an assignment… GOOD LUCK!! You'll end up pulling an all-nighter and then by the end of that you still might not be even done! Procrastination brings on so much more just unneeded stress and can really hurt your grade just because you made the one mistake of procrastinating.

Pull an all-nighter the night before a big test. My brain did not want to function at all and I ended up failing.

IF MY YOUNGER SIBLING WERE HEADING OFF TO COLLEGE, THE ADVICE I'D GIVE…

Go to class, don't skip. You get too far behind too fast.

Broaden your horizons and get involved in things that you might not have thought you would. By joining a club or going to a speaker you wouldn't normally go to you will see people from different cliques and expand your ways of thinking. (I know this is similar to your Bulletin Board Bingo, and although I don't do it on a monthly basis I do still browse the bulletin boards around campus and try to make it to a couple of speakers or events per month that I might not normally go to. It really is interesting to see the range of things offered for student entertainment at universities.)

Leave your game system at home. I saw my roommate and many others spend too much time in front of a video game, without such distractions you will find yourself more willing to go out and meet people, in addition to more time studying

Coming to college, the vast majority of your classmates have no idea who you are, don't know anything about your past, and are just as frazzled as you are trying to adapt to a new place. You get a chance to reinvent yourself. So, try new things, try new yous.

Don't be passive and think freshmen can't get involved. Give yourself a week or two and then find somewhere or create a way to contribute to the campus, you do not have to wait!

...take time to find what makes you tick, what excites you. Whether that is through classes, student organizations, etc.... get to know yourself!

Enjoy your time because it goes by too fast. Before you know it you are graduating!

Learn your limits. That applies not only to mind altering substances, but also to your limits with friendships, romantic relationships, etc.

Do not wait till the last minute on all of your assignments. It no longer works!

Don't say no (or yes) to something because you are nervous people will judge you. Do what YOU want to do. Sometimes you will learn from your mistakes — but most of the time you'll come out learning more than you could ever have imagined. Don't miss out on the fun social stuff. People who only focus on school are missing the best part of college. Make tons of friends and don't do something stupid that you will regret.

Don't worry about not making friends. You're at a school along with thousands of other people. You WILL find people who share your interests.

Stay away from Reddit.

If you were my younger brother or sister heading off to college, and I could give you one piece of advice, it would be to make your experience in college what you want it to be! Don't just sit there all year long and think "what if" for every opportunity that passes by! Just put yourself out there and try it out yourself! If an opportunity interests you, go for it! If you find out later it wasn't what you expected and you end up not liking it, then leave! At least you tried it out!

Focus on learning (Fun is for the weekend). Don't do the work to get it done, do it so you know it and understand it.

In some cases, former students offered feedback after they had completed all of their college years, and this is some of what they shared.

ACADEMICALLY, THE SMARTEST THING I DID OVER ALL MY YEARS IN COLLEGE WAS....

Not letting them corner me into a major freshman year. Many schools try to pressure you into one program of study and want you to decide as early on as possible in the process what you would like your major to be. While this is good and having a plan definitely helps, it sometimes, depending on the way the school runs things, will limit your abilities to take other classes and electives you might find interesting. By waiting a little while longer you will gain knowledge in many fields and make yourself more well-rounded and a better person.

Do papers when they are assigned, not the night before they are due. It is inevitable that it will happen a few times during your college life, but try not to. It helps a lot.

Chose a major that fit me and that I was interested in. College is so much more fun when you are look forward to going to classes instead of dreading it. I originally picked Mechanical Engineering as a Major and did not enjoy the classes, not enjoying the classes soon lead to not enjoying life. After switching to Computer Engineering Technology I found that I not only enjoyed and looked forward to going to class, but I enjoyed and looked forward to life. So the smartest thing you could do academically is to pick a major that you enjoy, and don't be afraid to switch a few times until you find the right one.

Learn which assignments were necessary. (I really wish this answer were: "learn wonderful study habits!".) As important as the academic aspect of your college experience will be, reading every word of every reading your professor ever gives you is not going to enrich your experience. I promise. I gave this piece of advice in a new student panel and my boss (I work for the Campus Activities Office, a division of Student Life) just kind of stared at me like I had handed out the phone number of the best pot dealer on campus. But I swear, this is really vital. I know what I need to do to get what I need out of a class. I know what I need to do to finish my papers and projects in a way that satisfies both my professor and myself. And I know what I can toss aside to complete another assignment, or do something fun and silly with my friends, which is infinitely more important.

Set up study times that were non-negotiable, speak to my professors and find out how to learn effectively, always leave time to relax/workout and go out with friends.

..... to be disciplined with my studies. I kept academics a priority in my life. It didn't eliminate my social life; I felt I had a good balance of the two. But when I look back, I have no regrets about my performance in the classroom and I know many people that do have regrets... I can't imagine that that feels good.

I switched my major because I wasn't enjoying what I was studying. I went from dreading my classes to actually enjoying them and looking forward to what I was going to learn next! I also took a chance and studied abroad in a place that not all of my friends were going (Greece). It was an experience that no one can ever take away from me!

Concentrate on my interest and excel regardless of its practicality. Also go to office hours. Instructors love thinking beyond the classroom and office hours visits tell them you've developed or have a previous interest in the material or subject.

Time management. If you don't know how to manage your time your college experience will not last very long.

Keep a notebook with important things that I will probably require later on in life.

Visit the tutoring center when I needed help, and going to see my professors. Sometimes the tutoring centers are better (like for Computer Science), and other times the professors are better (like Math).

Academically, the smartest thing I did over ALL my years in college was again, being overly organized about all my notes and managing my time well! Even back in high school I was the most organized and time management obsessed person in the school. But once I entered college, that wasn't even enough! You really need to be able to manage exactly what is going to get done and when!

Setting self-imposed deadlines for getting work done, talking with peers about problems.

Well, I've only had a year, but probably forming study groups that were serious about the class. Having help around is a lot better than just looking stuff up on the Internet. You will get distracted.

SOCIALLY, THE SMARTEST THING I DID OVER ALL MY YEARS IN COLLEGE WAS...

Maintain good relationships with my roommate. You live in close quarters with this person and if you do not get along and maintain a decent relationship with them it can make the whole experience much tougher. Having a roommate as a friend and confidant rather than someone you may not get along with is something that helps get through the tough times because you have someone to talk to right there to listen and to help.

Get involved with clubs. Contact friends at other universities and meet new people. Go out and have a good time, but don't be stupid. Meet a lot of people, it makes your time at college so much better.

Live communally in an interest house. Besides learning to cook (for 13!) and learning to share a space, I really learned how to share myself. We were (and are--five of the seven now-seniors are sharing a quint this fall, we all get together for dinner a couple of times a month) a family--with all the good and bad associated. Lots of long talks about socially ingrained privilege, and lots of long fights about who's doing dishes. To apply that to a community without interest houses or similar opportunities, I guess just put yourself out there, challenge yourself to meet different people, get out of your comfort zone, and try someday to cook for 13 people.

Being friendly and approachable goes a long way on campus. Allowing myself to get past appearance and demeanor led me to people I will keep in my life beyond graduation.

.... get involved in organizations that you believe in or are passionate about. I believe that is the greatest way to meet people because, typically, those people will have similar values to you. Therein, you will have a greater probability of developing a connection with them that will develop into meaningful friendships.

I switched my group of friends because they were not who I wanted to be associated with. Now they are my second family and I know they will always be there for me. The people before were too superficial to even understand that.

Maintain my friendship with my floor mates, they are all different majors than I am and so it helps me to branch out outside the college of science.

Not have too many boyfriends (or girlfriends). Exes are not fun. Trust me.

Get out. Become friends with the professors and tutors. And try not to piss people off.

ANYTHING ELSE?

Build as many friendships as you can in your early years because these people will be the ones that you are friends with or be the way to meet new friends throughout your college experience. (networking)

Join club or organizations

Go ahead and talk to the boy/girl that you think is out of your league.

Take advantage of opportunities you are offered, it can change your life

Know the history and the layout of the school

Become involved in student government

Get to know the town outside of the college this especially includes the great places to eat. Check out the small diners that are often found on main streets of downtown. In all of my travels these are usually the places with the best food.

If you have a roommate set up expectations for each other. Especially cleaning, sleeping hours and boyfriend/girlfriend rules

Figure out how long you want to go to school and then plan how you are going to get it done but don't be afraid to stay longer if you are given opportunities (A lot of good students take 5 years to get a 4 year degree)

Spend your money wisely

You can go out and have a good time but don't be stupid and most importantly don't drive home

On the same note, don't be afraid to be the DD, it gains you respect and it is often times hilarious

Take some fun classes that interest you. I was able to take a class on the history of country music and Assassinations of the 20th Century

Talk to your professors after class, they are people too (with a few exceptions)

Be proud of your school and make your school proud.

If your school offers a career fair, go to it, interview for as many internships/jobs as you can. On the same note, build up a strong resume. Document everything you do in college that can be put on your resume. This experience is invaluable as you get older.

Volunteer.

GO TO CLASS because you pay for them whether or not you go

I didn't get a part time job until 2nd semester of my freshmen year so you can get adjusted to college life

If you have the time I would recommend getting a part time job, it gets your mind off of schoolwork and you have the opportunity to meet more people.

Don't be afraid to change direction in your educational experience

If you have to buy books look to your friends first, then online, and than last but not least go to the bookstore. The only year I ever bought books before the first day of class was my freshmen year. The advantage of waiting is to see if you are actually going to use the book in class, if you have friends that you can share the book with or if you absolutely need the book.

Try not to get arrested.

Most of all have fun, it doesn't take long once you graduate to look back at college and wish you were there again. I am 86 days out of school and I already look back and smile at the "good ol' days"

As far as advice goes- you gave me a piece of advice many years ago that has been applicable to many areas of my life- and I reiterate it now…"slow down," you said. I recall this was in reference to my assumption that upon high school graduation my life would "take off" and I would grab the world by it's horns.

The reason I think this is applicable during the early stages of college is due to the fact that a huge amount of responsibility is suddenly given to each of the students and consequentially many fail to embrace this new freedom in a positive way. Being ambitious and getting involved are not opposites of this advice. However, not taking the time to ask one-self if this makes sense and humbly admitting that smart choices, most of the time, are tough choices and therefore require deep thought and reflection.

There is something to be said for being patient and taking one day at a time- not allowing life to overwhelm us; as freshmen year can certainly be overwhelming, at times. "Rome wasn't built in a day"- as the cliché admits.

Quick and practical tips: don't forget things like Q-Tips and band-aids because everyone does and when you need them, you need them; having the phone numbers of nearby delivery places will make you really popular at the tail end of parties/study sessions; parties/study sessions are not mutually exclusive if you're doing it right (okay, that wasn't so practical); go on an off-campus studies program--it will make you miss your campus a whole lot, and maybe you'll learn something.

College has so much to offer that will make you change your outlook and viewpoints, but this does not mean you have to lose who you are along the way. You can simply take this time as a chance to refine yourself.

It's a totally different lifestyle than in high school. Think carefully about the decisions you make, as the safety net you may have had at home probably isn't in place right off the bat during freshman year.

Here's my only advice for freshmen: YOU ARE SMART ENOUGH TO GET THROUGH THE FIRST YEAR. It might be hard, or it might be easy. It will be a substantial amount of work. Do it all, and study. You need to do the work to get the grade--there's no way around it. You can't just not do anything here. The rewards will be bigger than they appear at first, by the way.

Have fun. You're only going to be in a college for a little while. It'll be over before you know it. And this is where you truly make relationships that last a lifetime. So make sure they're good ones. Don't be afraid to fall in love. It's a beautiful motivator, but don't let it hinder your academics. And most of all don't be afraid to try something new and take risks. It's the only way to live life. Cheers!

———————————

Don't take crap from anyone, and don't be one of those who deals out crap to others.

———————————

Take your time in college and cherish every minute of it! Don't just be one of those students that will just sit in their dorm room or only talk to the people of their hall (whether you all are a "family" or not)! Be willing to try new things, to meet new people, and to just put yourself out there! If something catches your eye, try it out! In the end, you may end up surprising yourself because I know I did! Don't just sit back and watch as college passes you by. Take it and do as much as you can with it! You're only going to get out what you put into it.

My biggest bit of advice to freshmen is to be wary. While the opportunity presented at college is tremendous and also the rewards, it doesn't come free. They accept extra kids every year to weed out the weaker, dumber, less motivated, not as apt students so they get the best of the best. I had a terrible work ethic because my high school was a joke. Full college credit schedule since sophomore year, but it was easy. I almost got kicked out because I thought I could continue my old habits of B.S study and work ethic and I got nailed. The best thing you can do for yourself is to always put school work first and don't let college wear you down. It's a challenge, but if my lazy butt can do it, anyone can.

★★★

Thanks to all of you students who contributed here!

Alex	Ezra	Zach	Adam
Kali	Jill	Katy	Tyler
Brad	Karyn	Alex	Keelan
Brian	Kate	Koby	Max
Dustin	Seana	Ryan	Melissa

APPENDIX K:
HEY LOOK! HERE ARE ALL THE 'LOOK IT UPS!'
(WAIT... WHERE ARE THEY?)

Throughout the book, I peppered you with opportunities (commands?) to 'Look It Up!' The intent is to help wean you off any leanings you may have toward passivity. Although you're entering that time in your life when you need to take control of your own development and LOOK STUFF UP ON YOUR OWN, I'm not going to leave you hanging entirely.

All the 'Look It Up' links are collected on the *Carpe College!* website, so you can find 'em there:

carpecollege.com

Of course, you know the web is ever changing and as fickle as a first year college student (Wow! That may have sounded insulting). So, although these links were good and accurate at the time of printing, they may not be by the time you're reading. So, let me know if you find some bad ones. At least you'll have the general categories and you can LOOK THEM UP!

More important, this collection of resources should simply be a springboard to vault you further. If you encounter something you don't understand, look it up. If you're curious and intrigued by something, explore it in depth. Enough passivity already! (Especially if you're reading this in the summer with plenty of time on your hands.) Become an active, life-long learner and do your own research, damn it!

★★★

(Oh, and if you want to get all tech-fancy, use your phone on this QR Code to get you where you need to go.)

APPENDIX L:
A VERY POTTER GUIDE TO COLLEGE STUFF

(AKA A HOGWARTS HELPER THAT PROBABLY BELONGS IN A DIFFERENT BOOK, BUT I JUST COULDN'T HELP MYSELF AND HAD TO INCLUDE IT)

Now that you've experienced ye ol' grueling 'sorting hat' of college admissions, you've put all that 'early decision' and 'safety' talk behind you, and you actually know where you'll be in the fall, we'll move on to thinking about life at college... Potter style.

College... It's like Hogwarts. Yeah... but different.

Harry Potter and the Source of the Moan
Yes, you will encounter sex in college.

Harry Potter and the Chamber of Secretions
It's called the bathroom down the hall.

Harry Potter and the Prisoner of Ask Your Mom
That guy or girl who can't seem to cut the cord. Too much mommy-texting.

Harry Potter and the Mob at the Dryer
The laundry room might be packed. Plan accordingly.

Harry Potter and the Order of the Pizza
Ye ol' stand by for your dietary needs.

Harry Potter and the Half-Dollar Prints
Printing costs sometimes aren't fair either.

KYLE LABRIOLA

is a cartoonist, illustrator and writer best known for his several online comic series.

You can find his work and read his comics at

www.kylelabriola.com

Carpe College

ABOUT THE AUTHOR

After a roller-coaster undergraduate experience, a couple of masters degrees and an uninspiring advertising career, Mike Metzler ventured into teaching, where he has found his bliss and earned praise from every corner. Now, having taught nearly two decades of high school and college combined, Mike has learned a few things about the challenging transition from high school to college life, and he's eager to share his insights in *Carpe College!*

WHAT MIKE'S STUDENTS HAVE SAID....

You made learning fun, different, enlightening, and treated us like adults • Mr. Metzler is the reason I'm alive. This hero truly saved my life • Metzler loves his job, and it really shows • Thank you for encouraging us to reach outside ourselves and explore • In my list of inspiring educators, his name is at the top • There are few people who really get through to stubborn, obstinate, annoying, frightened teenagers; you got through to me • He really makes us think for ourselves • I feel better knowing there's a teacher like him • I am a life that was changed • Until I stepped into your class, I was taught 'the one right point of view' and just accepted what I was told • Thank you for being the best teacher I've ever had! • I feel lucky to have had the opportunity to know you and learn from you • Your class was a tough one, but only because you would never let us sell ourselves short of what you knew we had • You accepted nothing but our hardest efforts • You encouraged me to reach beyond my limits • You are a teacher we will all remember forever • I am a better person having known you • A teacher who dares to change "the way it is" and always believes in us students • You have truly been an inspiration to me. I will never forget you • I have always looked forward to coming to your class • You have been the most intriguing teacher – my all-time favorite – no lie! • You taught me to be excited when my thoughts differ from others, and you simply taught me to think better • Your passion makes us want to learn • Whatever you've done with us, it worked! • The most enjoyable class of my high school career! • I would like to become his friend, not just his student • Mike is an amazing guy • He was a great teacher and his class was one of the only classes that I looked forward to go to • I would really like to continue being in his class for the next 5 years • He was very interested in helping us adjust to college life • Mike was really impressive and an amazing teacher. His style really allowed us to get comfortable with our new college environment • Thank you for being your wonderful self!

JOT YOUR NOTES HERE…

CPSIA information can be obtained at www.ICGtesting.com
Printed in the USA
BVOW07s1706301111B3

337732BV00001B/1/P